D1496045

ASH GLAZES

ROBERT TICHANE

Illustrated with ceramics by Thomas Clarkson

Krause Publications, Iola, Wisconsin

Copyright © 1998 by Robert Tichane
Previously published in 1987 under ISBN 0-914267-05-1.
Now back in print with an added color section.

All Rights Reserved
Published by

700 East State St., Iola, WI 54990-0001
Telephone 715-445-2214

Please call or write for our free catalog of publications. Our toll-free number to place an order or obtain a free catalog is 800-258-0929 or please use our regular business telephone 715-445-2214 for editorial comment and further information.

No part of this book may be reproduced, transmitted, or stored in any form or by any means, electronic or mechanical, without prior written permission from the publisher.

Manufactured in the United States of America

Library of Congress Cataloging-in-Publication Data

Tichane, Robert
        Ash glazes

ISBN: 0-87341-660-0

1. Glaze   2. Pottery   3. Title

98-84626
CIP

Cover photo: Pitcher – 14" height, wheel thrown with textural slip and ash glazes by Thomas Clarkson

DEDICATED TO

Brother Daniel of Taizé, author and potter, working in the finest tradition of the Sung artists.

And, to the memory of Emil Wolff, author and scientist.

CONTENTS

SECTION I - INTRODUCTORY

SECTION II - MATERIALS

SECTION III - ADDITIONS AND SUBTRACTIONS

SECTION IV - SUBSTITUTIONS

SECTION V - TECHNIQUES

SECTION VI - OBSERVATIONS

APPENDIX

INDEX   211

Figure 1.1   Interior of contemporary Chinese wood fired kiln (Ching-te-chen).

1 INTRODUCTION

This book owes its inspiration to Brother Daniel of the Taizé Community of France. His fine text on Ash Glazes led me to think of expanding that work with some of my own observations, as well as with some extra information that was not available to him.

One of the extra pieces of information that I was able to locate was the two volume collection of ash analyses by Emil Wolff. This work was obtained by the Corning Museum of Glass Library (through the assistance of Virginia Wright and Sheila Tshudy) by means of an interlibrary loan from the University of New Hampshire. This monumental work was the main cornerstone of this book. In addition to this help, the Corning Museum of Glass Library, again through the work of Virginia Wright and Sheila Tshudy, obtained loan copies of several Masters theses. This assistance was of the type that allows new work to be accomplished, and to these people I extend my sincerest thanks.

Naturally it is also appropriate to extend appreciation to the authors of the several theses that contributed so much information and new outlooks to the theme of Ash Glazes. While there are undoubtedly numerous other Masters theses extant on the same subject, they have been neglected only through ignorance and not by intent. It is difficult to locate these sources in the first place, and even more difficult to obtain copies, since they are only printed in limited numbers and thus are gems to be protected.

The Alfred University College of Ceramics Library has been a treasure house for all of my work, and the cordial assistance rendered by the director, Bruce Connolly, and the library's staff,has made the job of collating data a much easier task. Their magnificent collection of ceramic literature is a must for anyone contemplating a search in the field of ceramics. In addition to the entire staff of the Alfred Ceramics Library, other people I want to thank are: John Bartoo, Dr. Fred Bickford, Dr. Robert Brill, Rena Brooks, Br. Thomas (Bezanson), Thomas Clarkson,

Louise Cort, Jean Gordon Lee, Robert Moes, Dave Pickles, Len Pruden, Dr. William Whitney, Wu Tung and Martie Young.

Nor can the importance of Bernard Leach to the field of ash glazes be over-emphasized. One only has to look for information about ash glazes in books published before 1940 (even 1950) to become aware that before Leach no one even mentioned the subject in the West. His was the cornerstone on which all later work was laid. Obviously, since then much has been done on the subject, and among others, I am particularly fond of Grebanier's work and Sanders' work.

In addition to all of the information obtained as described above, this book will concentrate to a large extent on a long series of experiments that I have run in an effort to confirm or refute some of the claims that are made for ash glazes. While the photographs of the samples (mostly plaques), which have been used to test the various theories and conjectures, may not always clearly illustrate the point that is being made, the mere fact that the point is **not** well shown may be as informative as any other piece of information. If you can't see any difference between the positive and negative examples, then perhaps the difference is not important to your work.

A happy consequence of any piece on ash glazes is that someone reading about them and experimenting with them should have a very high degree of success. This is in contrast to a subject such as copper red glazes, where the best glazes are balanced on a very precarious knife-edge of technique and it is even difficult for an expert to obtain consistent results. This relative ease in making classical ash glazes is in itself a snare however, because the artist attempting to make items which are unique to himself will be plagued by the problem that many ash glazes are very similar in appearance to one another. A lot can be learned by closely observing the several pictures in this book of the ware made by Thomas Clarkson. Mr. Clarkson has taken relatively simple ash glazes and applied them to finely formed and uniquely textured pieces and then topped this combination off with applied oxide colorants that produce a very distinctive modern ware. His ash glazed wares are anything but ordinary.

The main question today is: although we can make ash glazes without an excessive amount of effort, can we make ash glazed ware which is distinctive and also appropriate for both us and our times?

APOLOGIA:

I hope that you will forgive me an occasional slip in terminology. For example, there are undoubtedly a number of places where I have been careless in the use of terms, such as: soda and sodium and soda ash; or lime and limestone and calcium; or potash and potassium and potassium carbonate. If it seems important for your work, drop me a line in care of the NYS Glaze Institute, and I'll try to straighten it out.

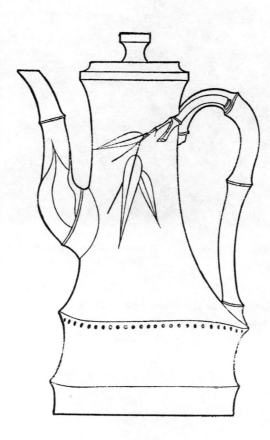

Courtesy of the Freer Gallery of Art, Smithsonian
Institution, Washington, D.C. 20560 (Acq. 52.10).

**Figure 2.1   Large Chinese jar of the Han dynasty (206 B.C.-221 A.D.).
Height 12 3/4".**

2   THE HISTORY OF ASH GLAZES

The history of ash and ash glazes is intimately tied up with the history of ceramics itself, and naturally must date back to the Chinese influence. This is because the Chinese were the originators of high fired ceramics and it is in this area that ash glazing is important.

Many other countries, in fact all countries, have heritages of **pottery**, which we can confirm thanks to the durability of fired ceramics. However, the historical finger points undeniably to China as the place of origin for the **high** fired ceramics which we call either stoneware, porcelain or proto-porcelain.

To find the earliest beginnings of high fired ceramics, we need to look for contrasts in the earliest notable civilizations, namely the Egyptian and the Chinese. And, it is more informative to look at the relics of their work rather than the remains of their writings, for the pieces tell the whole story if we are clever enough to read that record. From the sherds of Egypt and other countries of the Middle East we can see that there was no tradition at all for high fired ceramics; there was only pottery, no porcelain or even stoneware. In China however, there is a definite indication of a trend from pottery to fine porcelain over a period of 2-3000 years. Furthermore, the early high fired Chinese ware is the material that indicates the beginning of ash glazing.

The one regret that I have is that the workers in the field of art history have not been more thorough in their descriptions of the early glazes which involved the possible use of ash. There are certain clues which make it fairly obvious that an ash was used in a glaze rather than some **earthy** raw material. It would be nice to have this information to help determine just when ash glazes crept into the potter's bag of tricks. Of the many references on Chinese ceramics, Sato's work does the most thorough job of tracing the background of ash-type glazes.

If analyses of suspected ash glazes were available, then we might be on the lookout for the presence of the two elements phosphorus and manganese. The concentration of phosphorus in earthy raw materials is rarely more than a few tenths of a percent, while in wood ash the phosphate content may easily be several percent. Similarly for manganese, which is invariably present in earthy materials but only to the extent of a few tenths of a percent. In wood ash, manganese may be present in the range of 5-10% and almost invariably it is found in concentrations that are higher than those found for iron.

Another physical clue (which does not require analysis) is the thin glossy finish next to the glaze which appears whenever a soluble alkali is found in an applied glaze. Since ash contains a high percentage of potassium in the form of carbonate, it will produce this effect at the bottom edge of glazes where there is some bare body exposed. If we can observe, at a distance from the glaze, what the pure burned body looks like, and look at the body near the edge of the glaze, we can get an idea of whether soluble alkalies were present in the glaze slurry.

Without a specific, detailed description of what a potential ash glaze looks like, it is entirely possible that we can be fooled by the appearance of a plain mineral glaze. Such a glaze, with merely a high lime content, can look like an ash glaze when it is present on a stoneware body which has sizable amounts of impurities in it. I have taken a stoneware body and applied a thin wash of just calcium carbonate and have obtained a glaze with the same physical appearance as an ash glaze, namely dripping and beading. The coloring was slightly different, but if one considers that bodies vary to a great extent, and impurities in the earthy raw materials vary to a certain extent, then it seems likely that a simple mineral mixture could have been used to form some of the early glazes that we attribute to ash.

An intriguing aspect of the history of ash glazes is that in the Chinese background, the ash glaze was a transition glaze between the time when ware was merely burnished and fired and the time when it was glazed with a sophisticated mixture of limestone, feldspar, clay and silica. On the other hand in the Japanese (and also the American) tradition, ash glazes emerged with a life of their own. In Japan, ash glazing no doubt originated in a fashion similar to that in China, but it stayed around as a **folk** glazing technique. Next, as sophisticates began to admire the simplicity of folk art, it moved out as a distinct glaze type and was adopted by the "art" crowd.

And that is where we are today. At least I hope that we are artists! But that is why we must be careful with how we use ash glazes. They are not sophisticated glazes and I don't think that we should try to make them such. Also, I believe that it is an error to make a glaze with ash that looks like a glaze that could be mixed with normal glaze batch materials. It can also be a mistake to place rough ash glazes on artistically designed ware or on beautiful porcelain bodies. Ash glazes are peasant glazes that should be placed on peasant ware. If you ask, "Should only peasants be making ashed glazed ceramics," then I will plead the fifth amendment. [Actually, Tom Clarkson has proved just about everything I have said in this paragraph false. He has taken modern forms, used fine clay bodies, and by judicious use of texturing and coloring oxides, made beautiful, modern, ash glazed wares. That is artistry!]

Courtesy of Thomas Clarkson.

Figure 3.1 Contemporary ash-glazed Jar.

3   THE MINERAL CONTENT OF ASH

If you read an analysis of wood ash, such as one by Wolff, you might become confused, because he (as well as others) reports only certain oxides. He leaves out carbon dioxide for instance.

Therefore, as an indication of what the composition of wood ash really is, everyone should perform one simple experiment!

Take one teaspoon of wood ash, put it in a glass measuring cup, and then add one tablespoon of vinegar to the cup. This experiment will immediately show you whether or not there is much combined carbon dioxide present in wood ash in the form of carbonate.

Figure 3.2   Samples of ash in water and ash in vinegar.

My experience has been that when vinegar is added to the average wood ash sample, a great deal of carbon dioxide is liberated. And this is only to be expected. When wood is burned and ash is formed, much carbon dioxide is given off by the wood in the burning process. It is only natural that the ash residue, rather than being left as an oxide or a hydroxide, will become a carbonate through reaction with the available carbon dioxide. And, the carbonates of potassium and calcium (which are the most prominent basic materials in the glaze) will remain throughout the burning process since they do not begin to decompose until approximately 900°C (and most wood fires do not reach this temperature at the ash level). Therefore, unless the ash was fired under rather extraordinary conditions, we can normally expect that a good portion of wood ash will be present as carbonate.

On the other hand, one frequently sees analyses of wood ash in which no mention is made of carbonate in regard to the make-up of the material. For example, from Wolff's collection of wood ash analyses we would get the idea that no carbon dioxide is present in wood ash since he reports compositions as simple oxides, whose totals add up to 100% without the presence of carbon dioxide. Hence this question is a puzzler for us. Our acetic acid test proved that carbon dioxide is present in wood ash and yet we are confronted with analyses which add up to 100% and have no carbon dioxide in them. The worst part of this quandary is that it is not going to be easy to determine just how much of the alkaline material in wood ash **is** present as carbonate. This is because additional acidic components are present, such as chloride, sulfate, silicate and phosphate. The alkalies will, of course, be combined with these acidic components and in addition will be combined with the unaccounted-for carbon dioxide. For those of you who care, we will make two exact calculations and from then on merely make approximations to determine what the carbon dioxide content of wood ash will be.

For those of you who want a quick fix for the carbon dioxide question-- you may merely consider that one-third of a wood ash sample is carbon dioxide. This is a rule of thumb that will save you many calculations and will not leave you very far from the truth. Hence, whenever you weigh out a wood ash sample for a batch, multiply Wolff's numbers by 2/3 (or 0.67) to get values which can be used in glaze calculations. A fine book for information on calculating glaze batches is Ian Currie's "Stoneware Glazes."

CALCULATIONS

First, let us divide the analytical data on a sample of ash into three parts. The first part will contain the four alkaline elements, the second part will contain the neutral elements, iron and manganese and the third part will contain the four acidic elements.

I. A BASIC ASH - PINE WOOD ASH (according to Wolff)

Potassium Oxide	10.1%
Sodium Oxide	10.6%
Calcium Oxide	46.1%
Magnesium Oxide	13.5%
Ferric Oxide	4.8%
Manganese Oxide	—
Phosphorus Pentoxide	2.8%
Sulfur Trioxide	3.1%
Silica	8.4%
Chloride	0.7%
TOTAL	100.1%

After this we need to convert the percentage batch to a weight batch, and we can do this by considering the percentages as grams. Thus we have 100.1% equal to 100.1 grams. Next we have to convert the gram weights into mole weights, and we do this by dividing the gram weights by their respective molecular weights. And finally we need to convert these mole weights to the combining weights. For this we have to take into account the valence and the number of atoms that will be in the combined state to get everything into equivalent numbers. For example there are two potassium atoms in each molecule of potassium oxide, so the equivalent weight is half the mole weight. For calcium, there is only one atom of calcium in each molecule of calcium oxide, but each has a valence of two, therefore its equivalent weight is also one half of the mole weight. And so on for the rest of the elements.

OXIDE	Wt.	Moles	Equivs	True %
Potassium Oxide	10.1g.	0.107	0.215	6.7%
Sodium Oxide	10.6	0.171	0.342	7.1%
Calcium Oxide	46.1	0.823	1.646	30.7%
Magnesium Oxide	13.5	0.338	0.675	9.0%
Total Basic Equivalents			2.878	
Ferric Oxide	4.8	0.030	—	3.2%
Manganese Oxide	—	—	—	—
Phosphorus Pentoxide	2.8	0.020	0.120	1.9%
Sulfur Trioxide	3.1	0.039	0.078	2.1%
Silica	8.4	0.140	0.280	5.6%
Chloride	0.7	0.020	0.020	0.5%
Total Acidic Equivalents			0.498	
Net Basic Equivalents (basic–acidic)			2.38	
Carbon Dioxide (acidic)	—	—	2.38	(33.3%)
TOTAL	100.1 g.			100.1%

Now we can add up the acid equivalents and the basic equivalents in 100 grams of pine ash and see how they compare. We will neglect iron since it is practically neutral. Adding up the basics we find a total of 2.878 equivalents. Adding up the acidics, we find 0.498. Rounding these off and subtracting, the net result is a deficit of 2.38 acid equivalents. In other words if we were to neutralize 100 grams of **calcined** pine wood ash (oxides) with carbon dioxide, we would need 2.38 equivalents of carbon dioxide (or 1.19 moles or 52.4 grams of carbon dioxide) to neutralize the basicity which we have in 100 grams of this ash. This is because there are 44 grams in every mole of carbon dioxide and two equivalents in every mole. The natural form of pine wood ash would be the carbonate, since the normal furnace atmosphere is saturated with carbon dioxide. We shouldn't take these numbers too seriously, however, because there are also hydrates and hydroxides and bicarbonates in the mixtures, and to do a persnickety analysis of a wood ash sample would be a complete waste of time because of the variability of this raw material.

Converting the above numbers to percentages, we find that 100 divided by (100 + 52.4) equals 0.656 or 65.6%. Because of the unknown variables in the calculations, let us merely use 66.7% as a guesstimate whenever we see an analysis of "wood" ash that reports its figures as percentages of oxides and does not report the presence of carbon dioxide. By taking two thirds of the ash weight for the weight of all of the other oxides, we will have a ballpark figure for glaze calculations. In the last column of figures labeled "True" we have such a conversion—for instance, note that the original percentage of calcium oxide has been changed from 46.1 to 30.7 after it was multiplied by 0.67.

II. AN ACIDIC ASH - WHEAT STRAW ASH (according to Wolff)

Going through the same sort of calculation for another, different kind of ash (winter wheat straw), gives us a completely different result. This is because straw ash is acidic rather than basic like the ash from pine wood. Moreover, since there are no basic vapors available (equivalent to the acidic carbon dioxide gas) to convert the excess acid to a neutral state, the acid ash remains acid and what is measured as percent oxide is exactly what we get.

OXIDE	Wt.	Moles	Equivs.	True %
Potassium Oxide	13.7	0.145	0.290	13.7%
Sodium Oxide	1.4	0.022	0.045	1.4%
Calcium Oxide	5.8	0.103	0.206	5.8%
Magnesium Oxide	2.5	0.062	0.124	2.5%
Total Basic Equivalents			0.665	
Iron Oxide	0.6	0.004	—	0.6%
Manganese Oxide	—	—	—	—
Phosphorus Pentoxide	4.8	0.034	0.136	4.8%
Sulfur Trioxide	2.5	0.031	0.062	2.5%
Silicon Dioxide	67.5	1.125	2.250	67.5%
Chloride	1.7	0.047	0.047	1.7%
TOTAL				100.5%
Total Acidic Equivalents			2.563	
Net Acidic Equivalents			1.898	

Obviously there is more than enough acid in the wheat straw ash to neutralize all of the base, so the net number of equivalents will be of acid and they will amount to approximately 1.90.

This acid in the straw ash will not tend to react with components of the atmosphere, so we will not have to make a correction for carbon dioxide or anything else. There should be a slight correction for absorption of water from the air, but none of these calculations needs to be that precise. One assumption that we do have to make though, is that the ash has been fired to a high enough temperature so that all of the alkaline materials will have reacted with the acidics and that no free base is available. A temperature of 600°C should be hot enough to cause a reaction between all of this well blended material. I have added this final word of caution because I tried adding some vinegar to a sample of straw ash that I had burned myself. Imagine my chagrin when I found that some fizzing occurred. A further test with litmus paper also indicated that the original ash was basic in reaction. Fortunately when I tested a **refired** straw ash sample with vinegar it barely fizzed at all, so an inner reaction of the straw ash constituents must occur in order to produce an acid sample.

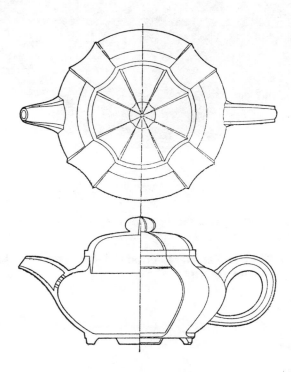

Courtesy of The Brooklyn Museum, Brooklyn, N.Y. 11238 (acq. 76.118).

**Figure 4.1   Japanese Sue ware jar, Nara period (7th-8th century A.D.).
Height 10 1/8".**

4 ANALYTICAL DIFFERENCES

Previously I warned you against taking decimal points too seriously in reading about the composition of ashes. Now we are going to take a more detailed view of numbers as they are recorded for ashes and ash glazes.

But, let there be no mistake on one point: I have nothing but the highest admiration for analysts. I have to, for I am one myself. However, we must also realize that there are limitations to chemical analysis and one of the limitations is involved with the human element. Each person is unique. Each person has a different cutoff point with regard to the amount of effort that he is willing to put into an analysis (or any other job for that matter). Just as some people will mow an acre of grass in one hour, others will take eight hours for the same task.

And this has to be, for in the real world each person has only so many hours to apportion and they have to be divided according to individual priorities. One must decide if one wants to work a whole lifetime on one project and just approach closer and closer to perfection. Some people do this—consider authors—Margaret Mitchell wrote only one book and it was a sensation. On the other hand Zane Grey wrote dozens of not-so-great books and yet he is famous too. Each man charts his own course and analytical chemists do too.

ANALYSES

So much for the philosophy of analysis, now for the nitty-gritty of analysis. There are a number of different ways to measure the amount of a component in a mixture or a compound. For the sake of simplicity let us take one example and look at it closely with the understanding that this will be true for every element in the ash mixture that we are considering.

For an example of analysis let us consider the element calcium, which is always present in quantity in ashes, especially wood ashes.

The mother of all analytical techniques is the so-called **wet** chemical analysis. This is an analysis often performed by the precipitation of a salt of an element. In the case of calcium the salt precipitated is commonly the oxalate. The salt is dried and weighed and the percentage of calcium is then calculated from the known composition of the oxalate. This is not a simple procedure though, and the difficulty of the work will depend on the mixture in which the original calcium was found. Thus there is no absolute result to be found because each sample is different. For instance, the amount of magnesium in a sample can complicate the determination of calcium, so the analyst must always be wary. As an example of what the pitfalls are, let me insert at this point a textbook direction for the determination of calcium by wet chemical analysis.

* * * * * * * * * * * * *

CALCIUM ANALYSIS

1. First precipitation: Prepare a solution that is free from silica, sulfur, the hydrogen sulfide group, and elements precipitable by ammonium hydroxide or ammonium sulfide. Dilute to 100-400 ml, and render the solution slightly ammoniacal. The solution should not contain more than the equivalent of 1 mg of CaO per ml in any case. Heat to boiling, and slowly add, while stirring, sufficient of a hot 4 per cent solution of ammonium oxalate to precipitate all of the calcium and to provide an excess of 1 g per 100 ml of solution. Boil for 1 to 2 minutes, and heat on a steam bath for one-half hour. Allow to cool, and filter at the end of one hour. Wash the paper and precipitate with five 10-ml portions of a cold neutral 0.1 percent solution of ammonium oxalate. Reserve the filtrate and washings if a determination of magnesium or a recovery of unprecipitated calcium is to be made.

2. Second precipitation: Dissolve the washed oxalate precipitate in 50 ml of dilute hydrochloric acid. Dilute, and add an excess of oxalate as in part 1. Heat to boiling, stir continuously, and slowly add dilute ammonium hydroxide until alkaline. Digest, filter, and wash as in part 1. Combine the filtrate and washings with those obtained after the first precipitation.

3. Ignition of the final oxalate precipitate: Wrap the moist precipitate in the filter paper, place in a platinum crucible weighed with a snugly fitting cover, and heat with the cover off or at the side so as to char but not inflame the paper. When the paper is fully charred, increase the flame, and, when the carbon has disappeared, set the crucible upright in the triangle, cover it, and heat at about 1200°C for 5 minutes. Throughout the heating it is well to protect the oxide from contamination by oxides of sulfur from burning gases or by volatile matter given off in muffles that are in general use. Remove the lid for a moment to permit escape of entrapped carbon dioxide, place the covered crucible in a desiccator containing sulfuric acid or phosphorus pentoxide, and weigh as soon as cool. The first weighing is a preliminary one and should be followed by a short ignition and a second weighing in which the weights are already placed on the pan and only the rider is quickly adjusted. A well-covered crucible containing ignited calcium oxide does not gain in weight during exposure for 1 minute under ordinary atmospheric conditions.

* * * * * * * * * * * * *

Impressive, isn't it! And I didn't even put in an equal quantity of footnotes that explained some of the finer points of calcium oxalate precipitation and ignition.

If this technique looks long and tedious, then you have gotten the correct idea. Chemical analysis is a tough job. The only way that wet chemical analysis is practical at all is when one analyst does a number of tests simultaneously and there is an economy of scale.

Although wet chemical analysis was the original method for doing determinations, many instrumental procedures are now available and they often speed up analysis greatly. For example, if you had the proper equipment, you would no doubt run a calcium analysis by an atomic absorption technique today. It is both rapid and accurate. Still, an interesting point to make is that each method has its pluses and minuses and no two give identical results from the same sample. And here is where I finally make my main point!

Any one analysis read in the literature may have been done by:

1. A world renowned analytical chemist,
2. Or, his underpaid assistant who was suffering from a hangover.

In addition, the analysis may have been run by:

1. A twelve hour wet chemical process,
2. Or, an estimation from emission spectroscopy done in ten minutes.

And finally, the original sample may have been:

1. Ash made from a carefully chosen sample of clean wood,
2. Or, it may have been ash made from wood burned on bare ground with the ash half mixed with dirt.

I am sure that you get the idea!

COMPARISONS

Now, as a final lesson, let us look at some numbers generated by the finest analytical laboratories in the world. In about 1970, W.T. Chase of the Smithsonian Institution in Washington, D.C., submitted standard bronze samples to 21 laboratories worldwide. The results of this test are very interesting and apply in principle to all fields of analysis. Some of the results are as follows:

Bronze Sample 1.	Copper Mean Value -	80.86%
	Range in Values -	75.4-83.5%
	Tin Mean Value -	14.72%
	Range in Values -	12-20%
Bronze Sample 2.	Copper Mean Value -	94.4%
	Range in Values -	89.6-97.46%
	Tin Mean Value -	2.96%
	Range in Values -	1.33-4.1%

Perhaps the most interesting facts about these results are that they were done on well mixed, uniform samples, by reputable laboratories, on relatively easily analyzed elements. The results of **ash** analyses—on diverse samples and on hard-to-analyze elements like silicon—would result in much greater variability.

Another difficulty in ash analysis is tied to the sampling problem. The analytical results can be no better than the original technique for selecting the sample. Sampling is the real limiting part of the analytical process. If the sample is not well chosen, then the numbers certainly cannot be worthwhile; this is a basic difficulty with **ash** analyses.

A particularly bad part of our dilemma is due to the quantity of organics that has to be burned to get a sizable amount of ash. This militates against the possibility that the analyses will be good, because you may have to burn 100 pounds of plants to get one pound of ash. Also, with ash that is obtained from a stove or fireplace, one wonders whether the ash came from some material that had grown for 100 years and other material that had grown for only 10 years. Also, was it mostly trunk wood or mainly branch wood; was there a lot of bark, or very little bark; and how much dirt and soil was trapped by the wood? For these reasons our samples are basically poor and the analytical results can be no better than these samples. Therefore I hope that you will agree with me when I use only very approximate numbers for analyses associated with ashes. Also, I hope that you have a lot of sympathy for the analysts who spent long hours over these specimens, with little knowledge of how good the samples were.

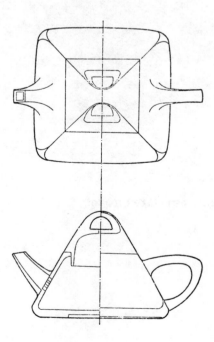

Figure 5.1   Contemporary ash glazed teapot.

5 THE VARIABILITY OF ASHES

One of the maximum benefits that can be derived from reading Wolff's book on ashes concerns learning of the variability of ash compositions. He not only reports on the composition of hundreds of ashes, but he indicates the range of compositions from different species, and also reports on the diversity within these species. Thus you may find, for example, that he lists 13 analyses done by different people on oak ash, and he reports the variation in potassium content is from 28-41%, the variation in the lime content is from 19-28%, the variation in the iron oxide content is from 0.4%-1.4% and so forth. And this gives a nice handle on what we can expect in natural ash and what our plans should be when we try to make a synthetic ash.

On the other hand, there are so many variables that affect the ash composition of plants that it would be presumptuous to try to evaluate all of them. Instead, I will merely give a few lists of ash compositions as reported in the literature. These will be grouped by category to illustrate how pronounced some of the differences are.

SPECIES

Obviously the **kind** of plant will have an effect on its ash composition. A tree ash would be expected to have a different composition than sugar beet ash for instance. Still, there are classes of ash that follow to some extent the classes of plants. For example, the ashes from deciduous trees will be closer to each other in make-up than they will be to the ashes from cereal grains. This is the characteristic that led Brother Daniel to propose groupings for ashes, depending on their silica content. He rates wood ashes as a group that is high in alkaline elements and straw ashes as a group that is high in silica. This is evident in the following table:

	Beech Ash	Oat Straw Ash
Potash	30.9%	26.4%
Soda	2.0%	3.3%
Lime	28.9%	7.0%
Magnesia	11.8%	3.7%
Iron Ox.	1.1%	1.2%
Mang. Ox.	5.3%	–
Phosphate	14.7%	4.6%
Sulfate	2.9%	3.2%
Silica	2.4%	46.7%
Chloride	0.1%	4.4%

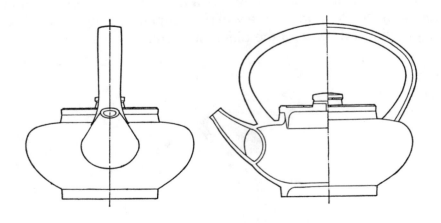

It is also logical that there will be different compositions for different parts of a single plant. The following table will illustrate this for ash from different parts of an oak tree. The same would hold true for the seed, stem, leaf and root of oats or any other species.

	Bark	Trunk	Branches	Leaves
Potash	5.7	45.7	8.1	33.1
Soda	0.4	13.8	3.1	—
Lime	89.1	24.0	51.0	26.1
Magnesia	2.7	2.9	9.1	13.5
Iron Ox.	0.5	1.8	1.2	1.2
Mang. Ox.	—	—	0.5	6.6
Phosphate	0.6	3.5	11.2	12.2
Sulfate	0.5	3.4	1.7	2.7
Silica	0.4	4.9	1.2	4.4
Chloride	—	—	—	0.1

AGE OF THE PLANT

As a plant matures, its composition changes throughout its body. Here are some analyses taken of the trunks of oak trees of varying ages:

	20 yrs	50yrs	345yrs
Potash	34.8	33.2	45.7
Soda	2.4	8.3	13.8
Lime	22.4	29.9	24.0
Magnesia	16.5	6.9	2.9
Iron Ox.	0.6	1.5	1.8
Mang. Ox.	2.7	0.6	–
Phosphate	17.0	11.5	3.5
Sulfate	2.8	2.1	3.4
Silica	0.7	5.2	4.9
Chloride	0.3	–	–

ENVIRONMENTAL EFFECTS

It would be nice to be able to compare the ash content of a tree species grown in a warm, sunny and dry climate with the same kind of tree grown in a cool, cloudy and moist climate, but the best I could find was this comparison of beech tree ash from Altenburg and Berchtesgaden. The former location is in a farming district of Germany, while the latter town is in the Bavarian Alps. These numbers show large swings in composition due to a cause that we might have expected to yield minor changes.

	Bercht.	Alten.
Potash	12.5	18.3
Soda	0.6	0.8
Lime	64.0	40.7
Magnesia	14.1	4.8
Iron Ox.	0.9	2.3
Mang. Ox.	0.2	13.0
Phosphate	2.8	10.4
Sulfate	1.8	1.8
Silica	2.2	5.2
Chloride	0.1	0.1
Alumina	0.8	1.1
Titania	0.2	0.1

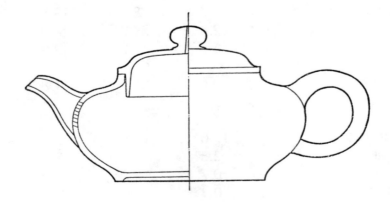

It would be helpful if we could guarantee that all of the previous numbers were significant and meaningful, but we know that there are a lot of unknown factors entering in each analysis, not the least of which is the sample selection and preparation. Before fastening your hat on any of the above results, just consider the following data from Wolff on the variation in numbers for the analyses of winter wheat straw ash in 18 samples (which should have been fairly consistent):

	Average	Range
Potash	13.7%	9.5-27.4%
Soda	1.4	0.0-7.3
Lime	5.8	2.7-8.9
Magnesia	2.5	1.3-5.2
Iron Ox.	0.6	0.1-1.2
Mang. Ox.	–	—
Phosphate	4.8	2.2-8.9
Sulfate	2.5	0.7-5.6
Silica	67.5	49.6-72.5
Chloride	1.7	0.0-7.4

Courtesy of The Brooklyn Museum, Brooklyn, N.Y. 11238 (acq. 74.111).

Figure 6.1 Japanese 17th century Tamba ware tea jar. Height 10 7/8".

6 ASH PERCENTAGES OF PLANTS

There is definitely a wide percentage difference in the amount of ash that will be left after calcining various plants. Some organic materials when burned will produce ashes which amount to only a few tenths of a percent of the initial dry weight of the organic material. On the other hand there are some plants or parts of plants which produce over ten percent ash. For example, if one burns only the white portion of the trunk of an oak tree, approximately one half of one percent of that material will remain as ash. On the other hand, when some types of straw are burned, they will yield eight percent of ash from the original dry weight.

Figure 6.2   A comparison of the ash generated from 100 g. of wood and 100 g. of straw.

And, as Brother Daniel has pointed out, this percentage weight can be a help when one is trying to identify the kind of ash which results from combustion. He has observed that if the percentage of ash is high, then it is probable that the ash will contain a high percentage of silica. And conversely, basic ashes will be the result when only a small percentage of ash is obtained from the combustion of an organic material.

Some of the materials which furnish a considerable amount of ash and which are high in silica are the grasses–although the same cannot always be said for hay. While this may be confusing to those of us who are not botanists (and who call anything which grows in a field a grass), the difference is due to the presence in hay of lupines like alfalfa, and cruciferous plants like wild mustard. However, for pure plant stands of Kentucky blue grass, timothy, Bermuda grass, and the like, one expects a high percentage of silica. Also, straws will provide a large amount of silica and a large amount of ash. This is true whether we are speaking of rice straw, wheat straw, rye straw or whatever.

For example, a wheat straw can provide 4% ash, of which 66% is silica. A barley straw can provide 4.4% ash with a silica content of 54%. Even corn stalks, with 5% ash, contain approximately 30% silica. And for rye straw, an ash content of 4.8%, with 56.4% silica, is reported.

On the other hand, the trunk wood of the beech tree has only half a percent ash with a 5% silica content. A fir tree is reported to have 0.2% ash with a 5.3% silica content. An olive tree has 0.4% ash and 3.8% silica content. And a mulberry tree is reported to have 0.4% ash in the trunk and 3.4% silica in the ash.

There are exceptions in most categories, but as far as generalities for ash are concerned, it is a pretty good rule, that: wood gives low percentages of ash with a low silica content, while straws and grasses give just the reverse. The most important thing to remember, though, is that hay is not straw and that the mixture that generally results from the harvest of a hay crop is apt to be a conglomerate of several different types of ash and will be quite different from the type of ash that you might expect from cropping a field that is pure Kentucky blue grass or pure timothy grass.

TABLE 6.1 (Wolff)

Material	Percent Ash
Beech Wood	0.46%
Oak Wood	0.49%
Birch Wood	0.33%
Pine Wood	0.30%
Spruce Wood	0.21%
White Fir Wood	0.24%
Corn Stalks	5.3%
Winter Wheat Straw	5.4%
Summer Wheat Straw	4.5%
Oat Straw	7.2%
Winter Rye Straw	4.5%
Sorghum Stalks	3.7%
Cotton Stalks	2.8%
Ferns	6.5%
Reeds	4.1%
Timothy Grass	6.8%
Red Clover	6.9%
Alfalfa	7.4%
Meadow Hay	7.0%
Alpine Hay	3.5%
Beech Tree Leaves	7.1%
Oak Leaves	4.9%
Pine Needles	1.4%
Birch Leaves	3.5%
Willow Leaves	7.8%

Before making a foray into the field to collect samples that look particularly advantageous from a percentage yield basis, it is important to consider the density factor. While hay and straw and such materials seem to offer superior quantities of ash, one should remember that they are bulky substances. This was brought home to me when I tried to burn a bale of straw for its ash. While the bale weighed about 50 pounds and should have yielded about two pounds of ash, it seemed to take forever to burn, at a pound at a time, and somehow the yield didn't come up to expectations. Sam Azzaro made a similar comment with regard to his efforts. He burned a small truckload of corn stalks and ended up with only a few hundred grams of ash. It is much easier to burn wood than hay or straw or leaves, and it is even easier to make an effort to locate an enterprise that is using scrap wood as a fuel!

Incidentally, Brother Daniel made a very pertinent observation in regard to ash from hay or straw. He said that when the hay crop is bad, this may be good for the ceramist, for the farmer may discard hay that has been spoiled because of mold from damp weather, and yet if this is burned to an ash, the potter can make use of it. Unfortunately, at the present time there are so many restrictions on open burning that it would be difficult to convert baled hay to ash for the sole purpose of making ash for ceramics.

7 WOOD ASH COMPOSITIONS

If you have a compelling urge to learn everything you can about the chemical composition of wood ash, there are two good sources available. The simplest course would be to look up data in the book called "The Dictionary of Applied Chemistry," by Thorpe. I think that the most recent edition is that of 1937. Under the heading of ASH, starting at page 503, he has a good selection of the ash contents of various vegetable materials derived from Wolff's work. If you have an irresistible desire to know **everything** there is to know about every kind of ash (as far as chemical composition is concerned) then by all means you should make an effort to obtain Emil Wolff's book called "ASCHEN ANALYSEN." The first thing, though, is that you should have a reading knowledge of German to make use of this book. And secondly, you will need a strong constitution, because the amount of data collected by Wolfe and placed in this book is so mountainous as to be mind boggling. In the 1880's and before, when there was a great deal of interest in fertilizers and their effect on plants, there was much work done on the inorganic chemical analysis of ashes of diverse plants. And Wolff made a very complete compilation of all the data accumulated before his publication date of 1880.

As an indication of the completeness of Wolff's work, here are some of the categories listed under the section on Ashes from Animal Products: cow's milk, sour milk, sheep's milk, camel's milk, dog's milk, pig's milk and human milk. And then he goes on with analyses of the ash from all of the many cheeses, and so on. If ashes are your game, then Wolff is your man.

The main conclusion that one would draw after scanning through Wolff's book is that if the material wasn't listed there, then it hadn't been invented yet. Still, I have noticed one exception. It appears that by 1880 no one had done an analysis of the ash from rice straw. Rice grain and rice chaff, yes, but rice straw, no. (Probably because not much rice was raised in Europe at that time.) And that is one item that we would like to know about for calculations on Oriental glazes. Still, we can make a rough extrapolation using values for rye, wheat, barley and oat straw ash. Also, Sanders gives an analysis for rice straw.

Actually, there are other data missing too. For instance, recently I read an Australian book on glazing by Ian Currie and in this book he lists the ash content of some of the trees common to Australia. On that continent it seems that half of the trees are some variety of Eucalyptus, with no mention being made of northern species such as oak or maple. Of course on the subject of Eucalyptus tree ash Wolff is silent. Hence if you have a source of an unusual ash, you may have to go further than Wolff's work. Fortunately many analyses have been made since 1880.

It is regrettable that Wolff's book does not have all of the data listed on how the samples were collected, how they were analyzed, etc. But this would have made it an impossibly long work and he does give the original references, so we can refer to them if necessary.

This chapter will deal only with wood ash. Other chapters will deal with other kinds of ash. Since the information from Wolff does not include particulars of ash other than chemical, this additional information will be left to other chapters also. Here we will only deal with the bare chemical aspects of analysis.

I will not be at all critical of the information presented by Wolff for two reasons. In the first place, it would be impertinent to criticize someone who has done such a magnificent job in collating all of this information, and in the second place, it would probably be moot, because the variability of ashes makes it unimportant to analyze any one sample to the nth degree. (In fact, one of the most valuable parts of Wolff's book is a large section which indicates the variability that analysts have found in chemical analyses for one variety of material.) Nor will I give an exhaustive survey of materials, because one of the aims of this book is to indicate that we should merely accept a rough indication of the composition for the ash which we collect, since in most cases we will be unable to get good chemical analyses on all of the components which are present in any one sample of ash. In fact, unless we had a collection of 100 pounds of ash (which might represent the residue from 5 TONS of wood), we wouldn't have a sample that would be worth analyzing from an economic viewpoint. And this will very seldom be the case for an average potter. Even if he could stand the frightful expense of the analyses ($100), he would seldom be able to collect a uniform sample of 100 pounds of ash.

As far as my personal experience is concerned, the only analytical instrument that I have used is the x-ray equipment on a scanning electron microscope, which gives a rough idea of the composition of materials. It currently has a lower limit of sensitivity of about one percent, so that if you have manganese or titanium at a level of a few tenths of a percent, those elements won't even be detected, although two tenths of a percent of titanium would have a profound effect on the color of reduced iron in a glaze. It is a useful instrument though, because it tells you what things you do not have—for example it lets you know when you **do not** have 5% of lead or barium in a glaze. And it does indicate when you have significant amounts of sulfur, chloride, or phosphorus in an ash. In fact, that was the most significant result that I learned from this

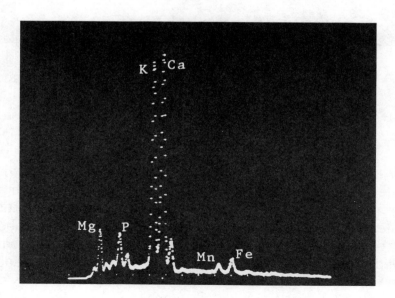

Figure 7.1 EDXR plot of mahogany wood ash.

type of x-ray analysis. There are not a lot of weird elements floating around that might give you exotic results. Most of the ancient Chinese glazes for example, are very straightforward, with few possibilities for strange elements. Their wares may have been obtained by unique firing conditions or unusual combinations of glaze and body, but they were not the result of the use of rare earth oxides, or barium, or strontium, etc.

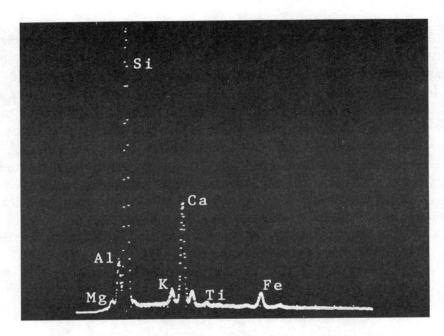

Figure 7.2 EDXR plot of Chinese Yueh ware glaze.

One of the questions that a non-technical person may ask is: how accurate are the analyses themselves? Did they know enough about analyzing materials in 1880 so that we can be confident of the results? Let me state that there should be no question in anyone's mind about the quality of the results from that era. By the 1880's most of the techniques for wet chemical analysis were well established, and the large supply of manpower led to meticulous work. Obviously at that time they did not have good techniques for doing alkali analyses, but I have the feeling that the skill of the workmen, even using a difficult procedure would allow the results to be reliable. The analysis of potassium, instead of being done by flame photometry, as would be the case today, would have been done by a gravimetric method—perhaps by chlorplatinate precipitation. And then sodium might be done by difference. I do think that the analytical methods would in all cases be well within the needs of the samples, considering the variability of ashes and woods.

As far as identification of materials is concerned, an oak tree in Europe and an oak tree in America would be the same as long as the species was the same. They were identified by their Latin names in Wolff's book although I will not go to that length to identify them here.

The thoroughness with which some of these analyses were done can be exemplified by the following case: this is the average of 6 analyses of beech wood (50-90 years old) and its ash, reported by Wolff. In the wood there was a 0.43% content of ash oxides (neglecting carbon dioxide). When the ash was analyzed, the following average composition was reported: 28.6% potash, 1.9% soda, 37.7% lime, 11.2% magnesia, 1.3% iron oxide, 5.1% manganese oxide, 6.8% phosphorus pentoxide, 1.4% sulfur trioxide, 6.0% silica, and 0.01% chloride. This is a good "representative" composition for unwashed wood ash. If you wanted to take one group of numbers for an "average" wood ash, this would be an acceptable set. When you weigh out ash which contains carbonate (which is normally the case), just multiply the above numbers by 0.67 to obtain the corrected percentages.

Each one of these numbers was reported by Wolff to one additional decimal point, But I have rounded them off to only one decimal point because of my objection to reporting non-significant figures. I cannot believe that the analyst was capable of analyzing potassium oxide to the accuracy implied by the figure of 18.42%. I will believe 18.4%, but not any better than that. My seeming inconsistency in first saying how good their analyses were and then criticizing their final accuracy is not as bad as it sounds. It is a frequent habit of authors to carry one more decimal point than is warranted and that is the practice that I am criticizing here. Extra decimal points are still being thrown around with abandon today and it is just as reprehensible in a US economic projection as it is in reporting chemical analyses. Let's just say that after seeing a 3.7% growth reported for the Gross National Product and then seeing it changed to 2.9% one month later, that I am not too impressed by anyone's numbers. Today, people with calculators and computers tend to report decimal readings just as read on their machines without any consideration for their true accuracy, which is a very bad habit.

Taking another look at the numbers found for the average beech tree wood ash, Wolff also reports the **range** for the different values. In the case of potassium oxide, it is from 16.4-37.7%; for sodium oxide from 0.1-2.2%; for calcium oxide, from 36.2-49.5%; for magnesium oxide from 7.5-16.2%; for manganese oxide from 1.2-12.8%; for iron oxide from 0.0-2.7%; for phosphorus pentoxide from 4.4-9.6%; for silica from 3.8-7.8%; for sulfur trioxide from 0.3-3.2%; for chloride from 0.0-0.1%. Obviously there are wide variations in wood and ash compositions. This is a disadvantage in that there is obviously no "average" that we can hang our hats on and use as a typical ash composition. On the other hand, the bright side is that no one can disparage our synthetic ash compositions by saying that they are not like a natural ash. Almost any synthetic effort will be like **some** natural ash.

Seriously though, the points to notice in the above figures are the ranges in the colorants, the phosphates, and the alkaline materials, in about that order of importance. Can you imagine for instance the results that would occur from working one day with an ash containing 1% of manganese oxide and the next day with an ash containing 12% manganese oxide? With both ashes coming from the same variety of tree! At least with a phosphate range from 4-10% you could have opals in either case. And even though the alkalies and alkaline earth oxide change widely, they might tend to balance out by being, first high on one side and low on the other, and then the reverse.

A table of representative wood ash analyses from Wolff will be found in Table 7.1

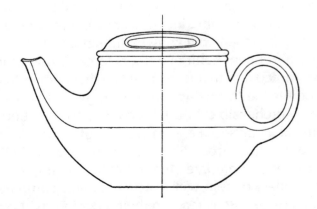

TABLE 7.1

AVERAGE WOOD ASH COMPOSITIONS (WOLFF)

WOOD	*K	Na	Ca	Mg	Fe	Mn	P	S	Si	Cl	#	%
Beech	28.6	1.9	37.7	11.2	1.3	5.1	6.8	1.4	6.0	0.0	6	0.43
Oak	34.8	2.4	22.4	16.5	0.6	2.7	17.0	2.8	0.7	0.3	13	0.49
Birch	23.6	2.3	29.0	16.5	0.9	8.7	14.7	1.7	2.0	0.7	6	0.33
Pine	14.3	1.0	53.6	10.7	0.1	3.3	6.1	3.5	2.6	—	7	0.30
Fir	21.8	3.6	29.3	16.9	1.4	—	18.0	5.7	2.7	0.6	3	1.80
Larch	23.6	1.7	45.1	13.2	3.0	—	7.7	2.1	3.2	—	6	0.17
Spruce	19.7	1.4	34.0	11.3	1.4	24.0	2.4	2.6	2.7	0.1	9	0.21
White Fir	39.9	0.9	11.1	9.6	0.7	28.6	6.1	1.8	1.3	—	2	0.24
Maple	14.4	0.7	63.4	5.9	1.0	0.5	8.5	1.9	3.8	—	2	0.98
Deciduous Trees	8.9	2.4	71.5	5.3	1.8	0.3	4.2	1.8	3.8	—	11	0.36
Trees												
Horse Chestnut	25.7	—	43.0	4.9	—	—	19.2	—	2.6	6.1	—	0.80
Walnut	15.3	—	55.9	8.1	2.2	—	12.2	—	2.9	0.3	—	3.00
Mulberry	6.2	13.7	54.6	5.4	0.6	1.5	2.1	9.8	3.4	4.7	—	1.40
Willow	34.0	—	41.1	6.0	0.5	0.2	13.0	2.6	0.1	0.5	—	2.90
Orange	11.7	3.2	55.1	6.3	0.6	—	17.1	4.6	1.2	0.2	—	2.30
Olive	21.2	—	63.0	2.3	0.7	—	5.4	3.0	3.8	0.5	—	0.40

*Elements have been used as abbreviations for the oxides.

Courtesy of the Freer Gallery of Art, Smithsonian
Institution, Washington, D.C. 20560 (Acq. 01.65).

**Figure 8.1   Large Chinese Chi-chou ware bottle of the Sung dynasty. Deep brown
with mottling from ash splashes.**

8 STRAW AND HAY ASH COMPOSITIONS

In this chapter, Wolff aids us with plenty of numbers on hay and straw ash, but it is Brother Daniel who gives a helpful interpretation.

As an example of straw ash analysis, here are the figures that Wolff gives for an average of 38 samples of Oat Straw Ash. From these we can see what a beautiful raw material this is for glaze making. His average percentage composition for Oat Straw Ash is:

Potash	26.4%
Soda	3.3%
Lime	7.0%
Magnesia	3.7%
Iron Ox.	1.6%
Mang. Ox.	—
Phosphate	4.6%
Sulfate	3.2%
Silica	46.7%
Chloride	4.4%

This is really a unique material! Actually it is a glaze by itself, although one would like to add a little kaolin to it to raise the silica and alumina content. But, consider the presence of the 4.6% phosphate and the 4.4% chloride—these materials are going to give unusual results in glazes!

42

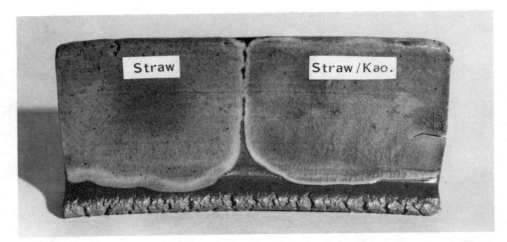

Figure 8.2   Two oat straw ash glazes on a test plaque, one with 10% kaolin. Both are transparent. Note some bleaching near the glaze borders.

(The reason that I selected an oat straw ash as an example instead of some other variety, is that in this section of New York State there are not many other straw generating materials that are raised, because of the harsh climate. When I go to the local feed store to get a bale of straw, it always turns out to be oat straw.)

As we said, in considering the composition of the above example of ash, it seems like a glaze all by itself. And indeed it has evidently been used for this purpose–if not for a base glaze, then at least for a decoration. The Chinese ware known as Chi Chou temmoku, (which was made a little to the south of Nanchang in Kiangsi province, back around the time of the Sung dynasty), was made of a dark brown (high iron) glaze decorated with applications of straw ash. In my attempts to duplicate this glaze and its decoration, I have tried many combinations and one of the best is an application of a straw-type ash over a brown glaze. In addition, I have found no other combination of ordinary materials which provides this same effect. So I see no reason to doubt that the Sung Chinese used straw or reed ash as an applied decoration.

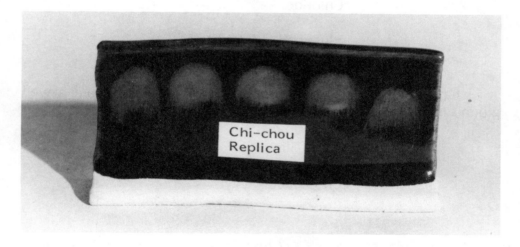

Figure 8.3 Replica of a Chi-chou type glaze, made with an Albany slip-containing base glaze, splashed with a synthetic straw ash slip.

The composition of the base glaze used by the Sung Chinese was found to be the following (as analyzed by Chen Xianqiu of the Shanghai Ceramic Institute):

Potash	5.1%
Soda	0.3%
Lime	8.0%
Magnesia	2.6%
Iron Ox.	4.3%
Mang. Ox.	0.9%
Phosphate	1.6%
Sulfate	—
Silica	61.9%
Chloride	—
Alumina	13.5%
Titania	0.7%

I have made an acceptable dark brown base glaze from a well ground mixture of:

Albany Slip	87
Whiting	10
Iron Oxide	3

An example of Chinese Chi Chou ware may be seen in the figure. It was apparently made by coating ware with an overall glaze having a high iron content, then applying a moist, cut paper decoration over the glaze, and finally spraying over this a straw ash slip. After spraying, the paper could be lifted off the article and the bowl could be fired. Other techniques were also used for decorating, including painting with an ash slip over the dark brown base glaze. The straw ash that the Chi Chou potters used was probably rice straw ash, which has the composition listed below (according to Sanders). It is higher in silica and lower in alkalies than oat straw ash, probably because rice is grown in a water culture. A composition which I made and which gave good spots is also listed.

Courtesy of the Museum of Fine Arts, Boston. William S. Bigelow collection (acq. 98.12).

Figure 8.4   Chinese Chi-chou ware tea bowl of the Sung dynasty with a cut paper design

MATERIAL	SANDERS	SYN. ASH
Potash	6.7%	37%
Soda	1.4%	—
Lime	5.8%	12%
Magnesia	2.6%	3%
Iron Ox.	0.5%	3%
Mang. Ox.	0.6%	3%
Phosphate	4.7%	8%
Sulfate	—	—
Silica	75.5%	31%
Chloride	—	3%

A batch for the synthetic ash above was:

Pearl Ash	30
Minusil-5 Silica	20
Dolomite	10
Bone Ash	10
Potassium Chloride	5
Iron Oxide	2
Manganese Oxide	2

The most remarkable thing about straw ashes (as compared to wood ash) is their high silica content. If we look down a list of various straw ash compositions (in Wolff's work), we see values such as: 43%, 29%, 47%, 51%, 54%, 49%, 47%, 67%, & 72%, for the percentages of silica in several varieties of straw ash. One must be just a bit cautious, though, because occasionally there may be a surprise. For example, Wolff reports that buckwheat straw ash contains only 5.5% silica.

But, Brother Daniel's technique for evaluating ash is so simple and so useful that it should be applied whenever you have the slightest doubt about your ash material. This is the technique of making a small button of an ash, firing it to 900-950°C, and then noting whether it remains powdery (wood ash) or whether it consolidates into a glassy mass (straw ash). [I mix ash with a cornstarch slurry, form it into a pellet, and then dry it thoroughly before firing it.] This is a nearly foolproof technique for recognizing a sizable amount of silica in the presence of a modest amount of alkaline material. If the silica is below about 10%, then the ash will usually remain powdery.

Figure 8.5 A comparison of two ash pellets fired to about 900°C. The straw ash pellet has fused, while the wood ash pellet remains friable.

Hay on the other hand is an entirely different situation (because of
its highly variable composition) and one must be very cautious when
using hay ash. Two examples of the ash content of different hays will
give an idea of this variation. First, let us look at an analysis for timothy
grass hay ash, as given by Wolff:

Potash	34.7%
Soda	1.8%
Lime	8.1%
Magnesia	3.2%
Iron Ox.	0.8%
Mang. Ox.	—
Phosphate	11.8%
Sulfate	2.9%
Silica	32.2%
Chloride	5.2%

This is a fairly typical analysis if one looks down a long list of various types of grass hay ash, just as the ash of oat straw was fairly typical of grain straw ash. The items to note about grass-hay ashes are: the slightly lower silica content (30% versus 50%); and slightly higher amounts of potash and phosphate. Timothy hay ash should fuse to a glassy button at 950°C, but it is low in silica compared to a normal glaze.

The danger of likening hay to straw is brought out more strongly by an examination of the ash of clover-type plants. Rather typical of the numbers reported by Wolff are these from the summary of 113 analyses on red clover. He finds the composition, on average, to be:

Potash	32.3%
Soda	2.0%
Lime	34.9%
Magnesia	10.9%
Iron Ox.	1.1%
Mang. Ox.	—
Phosphate	9.6%
Sulfate	3.2%
Silica	2.7%
Chloride	3.8%

It is obvious from this report that the ash of clover and plants of this family are much closer in composition to wood ash than they are to straw ash, because of their very low silica content. There is a difference, though, between clover hay ash and wood ash, in that the **amount** of pure ash resulting from burning clover is much higher than for wood. While wood ash represents perhaps 0.5-1.5% of the original wood, clover plants provide 5-8% of the original dry weight in ash. In the case of these 113 analyses, the average ash content was 6.9%. So if any single material had to be burned to generate an alkaline ash, I would suggest that one should hunt around for a farmer who has some surplus moldy clover hay that he wants to get rid of. Burning this material would give both a large quantity of ash and a high proportion of alkali.

Still, the emphasis in this chapter should be to **TEST**. Test your hay or straw sample via a button fired to 950°C. This will allow you to make a much more logical sequence of test glazes from an ash!

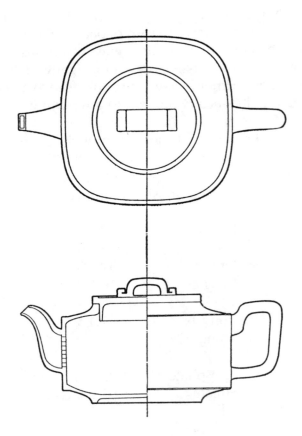

TABLE 8.1   GRASS-TYPE ASH COMPOSITIONS (WOLFF)

	*K	Na	Ca	Mg	Fe	Mn	P	S	Si	Cl	#	%
STRAWS												
Wheat	13.7	1.4	5.8	2.5	0.6	—	4.8	2.5	67.5	1.7	18	5.4
Rye	22.6	1.7	8.2	3.1	1.9	—	6.5	4.2	49.3	2.2	25	4.5
Oats	26.4	3.3	7.0	3.7	1.2	—	4.6	3.2	46.7	4.4	38	7.2
Barley	23.3	3.5	7.2	2.6	1.1	—	4.2	3.9	51.0	3.2	30	5.4
Corn	36.3	1.2	10.8	5.7	2.3	—	8.3	5.3	28.8	1.4	1	5.3
Soya	15.4	2.2	44.8	15.4	0.8	—	9.3	6.4	5.4	0.2	1	3.8
GRASSES												
Rye Grass	39.5	—	11.7	2.7	0.9	—	9.2	6.8	26.7	2.8	7	14.0
Timothy	34.7	1.8	8.1	3.2	0.8	—	11.8	2.9	32.2	5.2	9	6.8
Poa	43.6	1.8	12.0	2.5	1.6	—	9.4	10.5	16.6	2.3	1	2.7
CLOVERS, ETC.												
Red Cl.	32.3	2.0	34.9	10.9	1.0	—	9.6	3.2	2.7	3.8	99	6.9
White	21.5	7.2	30.2	9.5	2.1	—	12.8	7.4	4.5	4.2	4	7.3
Alfalfa	23.6	1.8	40.7	4.9	1.9	—	8.5	5.7	9.5	3.0	12	7.4
Vetch	27.2	1.3	52.0	4.6	1.3	—	8.8	1.4	3.2	0.9	5	6.4
Lupine	23.3	7.2	25.7	9.5	2.8	—	17.0	5.6	7.0	1.7	3	4.1
Fern	38.2	3.6	11.4	6.4	1.7	0.2	7.6	3.5	20.4	7.6	9	6.5
Reeds	17.8	0.7	7.7	2.7	1.9	—	5.3	2.3	59.7	3.6	4	4.1

*Elements have been used as abbreviations for the oxides.

Courtesy of Thomas Clarkson

Figure 9.1 Contemporary Ash glazed jar.

9 TREE LEAF ASH COMPOSITIONS

All kinds of leaves might have a potential for ash glazes, but the subject matter of this chapter will be **tree** leaf ash, because this is a raw material which is in good supply in the United States.

Although the use of leaf ash might be expected to be common because of the high yield of ash from leaves, it may not be as advantageous as some other ash materials. A sad fact about tree leaves is that they are much higher in potash content when they are green than when they have fallen from the tree. For example, Wolff reports that beech tree leaves in August have an ash content of 4.9% and a potash content of 20.2% (in the ash), while in November the beech leaves yield 7.1% ash and of that only 7.7% is potash. There is an increase of lime, though, from 29% to 40%. Presumably both yields were based on dried leaves.

For oak leaves, Wolff reports that the percentage of potash in green leaf ash is 33%, and in fallen leaves is only 3.4%. However, while this may be disheartening if you are looking for fluxes, it can be encouraging from the standpoint of the absence of soluble salts in the final glaze.

Since it is not likely that we will be using green leaves as a source of ash, we will only consider fallen leaves in this chapter.

For November leaves from beech trees, the results of 7 analyses are reported by Wolff to have an average of 7.1% ash, with an average ash composition of:

Potash	7.7%
Soda	0.2%
Lime	40.7%
Magnesia	4.1%
Iron Ox.	1.3%
Mang. Ox.	0.2%
Phosphate	5.7%
Sulfate	3.7%
Silica	34.6%
Chloride	0.3%

An outstanding feature of the numbers for tree leaf ash composition is a universally high lime content. When I ran three types of leaves using the EDXR unit of the scanning electron microscope, the same results showed up there. In each case the calcium content was higher than any other element. This can be seen in the following graphs:

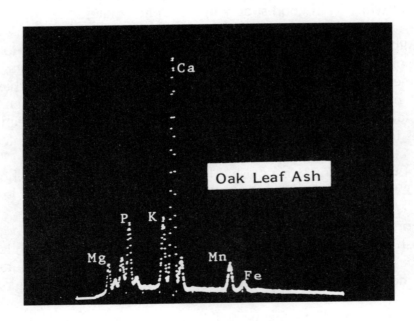

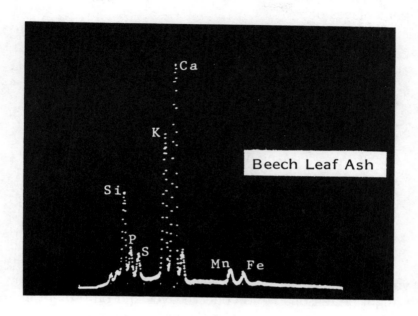

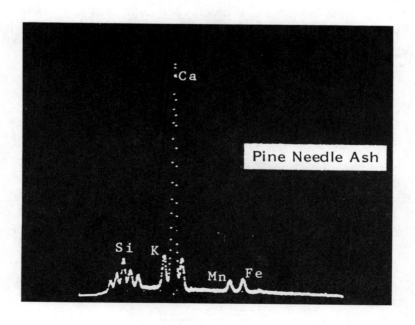

For oak leaves collected in November, Wolff reports 4.9% ash, with oxide percentages of:

Potash	3.4%
Soda	0.6%
Lime	48.6%
Magnesia	4.0%
Iron Ox.	0.6%
Mang. Ox.	–
Phosphate	8.1%
Sulfate	4.4%
Silica	31.0%
Chloride	–

If you happen to have a good Fall with lots of dry leaves and no rain, then it might be reasonable to collect leaves and burn them in a container such as the one described by Bessie Glover in her M.A. thesis at Eastern Carolina University at Greenville (at least as long as your local fire department and EPA people are not looking). Nevertheless, I think that normally, leaves will not be a practical source of ash for glazing. In this region of New York State, it always seems to rain just as the leaves begin to pile up. However, if you have no other source, then give it a try (legally).

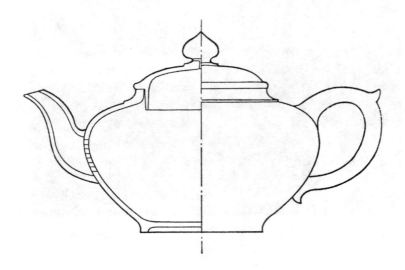

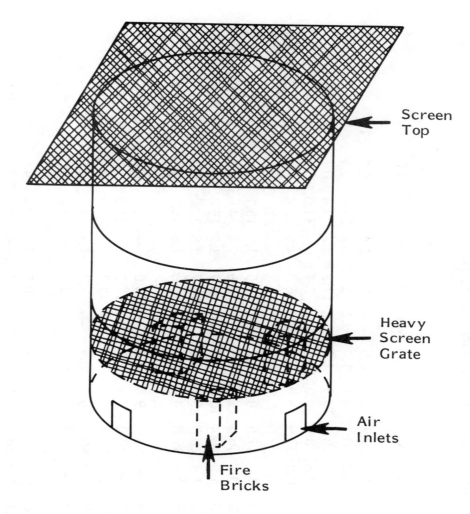

Screen
Top

Heavy
Screen
Grate

Air
Inlets

Fire
Bricks

Figure 9.2 Barrel-type burner of the kind described by Bessie Glover in her Master's thesis.

On the other hand, I think that leaf ash would lend itself readily to synthesis. It could easily be formed by mixing the fluffiest available powders of: silica, calcium carbonate, calcium sulfate, calcium phosphate and any other minor elements you might care to add. Then the well mixed batch could either be fired to 650°C or be used as the raw powder. [Test first, though, to make sure that it doesn't sinter on firing.] This should give a reasonable facsimile of a natural leaf ash and will save you all of the hours and problems involved with burning leaves.

TABLE 9.1

LEAF ASH COMPOSITIONS (WOLFF)

	*K	Na	Ca	Mg	Fe	Mn	P	S	Si	Cl	#	%
Beech, Aug.	20.2	1.6	29.1	7.5	0.9	1.0	8.4	2.4	28.7	0.1	13	4.9
Beech, Nov.	7.7	0.2	40.7	4.1	1.3	0.2	5.7	3.7	34.6	0.3	7	7.1
Oak, Aug.	33.1	—	26.1	13.5	1.2	6.6	12.2	2.7	4.4	0.1	1	3.5
Oak, Nov.	3.4	0.6	48.6	4.0	0.6	—	8.1	4.4	31.0	—	1	4.9
Pine, Green	30.0	0.8	23.9	6.9	7.0	7.4	16.0	4.8	3.4	—	8	1.9
Pine, Fallen	10.5	3.7	37.6	9.8	4.7	2.4	8.5	3.9	15.1	—	14	1.4
Fir Needles	1.6	0.7	66.3	12.2	1.5	—	8.6	5.4	4.0	—	5	3.5
Larch, Green	22.8	1.5	26.4	10.4	2.6	—	16.2	3.7	16.8	—	5	3.5
Spruce, Green	29.6	1.4	20.5	8.3	1.6	1.0	14.7	2.6	20.2	0.1	8	2.6
Spruce, Fallen	3.3	1.0	39.8	4.5	3.0	0.4	5.0	1.6	45.0	—	24	4.6
Walnut, Green	26.6	—	53.7	9.8	0.5	—	4.0	—	2.0	0.8	1	7.0
Mulberry	22.7	—	32.2	7.1	0.7	—	12.7	2.0	21.6	1.0	1	9.4
Birch	23.3	2.7	39.3	15.4	1.5	—	13.3	1.7	2.3	0.6	1	4.5
Orange	16.5	5.2	56.4	5.7	0.5	—	3.3	4.4	4.8	4.0	1	10.5
Olive	26.3	—	56.2	5.2	0.6	—	3.7	3.0	3.8	1.3	1	4.5
Lettuce	46.0	9.4	6.1	2.2	—	—	8.5	3.9	20.2	4.8	1	13.4
Cabbage	23.1	8.9	28.5	4.1	1.2	—	3.7	17.4	1.9	12.6	2	20.8
Spinach	16.6	35.3	11.9	6.4	3.4	—	10.3	6.9	4.5	6.2	2	16.5

*Elements have been used as abbreviations for the oxides.

10 WASHED ASH GLAZES

The field of ash glazing is neatly divided into two categories. One group of people use ash as received from the firing; the second group of people **wash** that ash before using it in their glaze.

Although I belong to the first group and use unwashed ash, the second group operates under some valid points. First of all, washing allows the elimination of unburned bits of wood and charcoal. Next, with washed ash, one does not have to worry about soluble alkali salts in the glaze slip. The difficulty with soluble alkalies is that they are absorbed by the body and during firing have a definite softening and color transfer effect in the body. In addition, they cause problems in mixing a glaze batch. The high alkalinity from the dissolved salts causes either flocculation or deflocculation, and either one of these can be a nuisance. Also, high alkalinity can adversely alter the functioning of other materials that are added to benefit glazes, such as thickening agents of either organic or inorganic type. The alkalinity of a raw wood ash glaze batch is very high and on a pH scale of 0-14, it is undoubtedly at least 12. One additional factor is that it is so alkaline that you would not want to put your hands in it for more than a quick dip. If you were glazing a long series of ware, you would definitely not want to have your hands in and out of the slurry for an hour.

But, there are two big problems with washing ash. In the first place the physical process of washing ash is difficult. You start out with a light, fluffy, voluminous material and then add a great deal of water to it, after which the remaining matte precipitate will have to be dried. And obviously, since the ash is very finely divided, it may not all precipitate readily in a short period of time. So the process can be very labor intensive and time consuming.

A second negative factor is the fact that some of the fluxing ability of wood ash is lost in the washing operation. One of the benefits of using ash in a glaze is its fluxing capability, and if ash is washed you may lose a fourth of the fluxing capacity. Then too, there is the problem of when to stop washing. Directions are often given to wash an ash until until the liquid is no longer alkaline, however this may be an extraordinary task if calcium oxide is present in the ash. Calcium hydroxide or oxide has only a limited solubility in water, so an ash that was fired above 900°C will definitely have a lot of lime or hydrated lime in it. In such a situation you could probably spend the next ten years trying to wash all of the alkalinity (from lime) out of an ash. Since lime is so alkaline it takes only a little of it to make a slurry alkaline. You could wash it and dissolve a little, and rewash it and dissolve a little more, and so on until you were blue.

If you must wash ash, I think that the best idea would be to give it one thorough washing with a large excess of water and then call it quits. This would probably remove 95% of the soluble alkali from the ash and would not cause you to use an excessive amount of labor in an effort to remove the last small amount of alkaline material.

The question also has to be asked: what are we removing from the ash and what are we leaving behind from the washing operation? For an examination of this, let's look at one average wood ash that has a fair amount of alkalies and a fair amount of alkaline earth elements in it. This could be a sample of beech wood ash whose composition is reported by Wolff to contain:

Potash	16%
Soda	3%
Lime	63%
Magnesia	11%
Iron Oxide	1%
Manganese Oxide	–
Phosphorus Oxide	3%
Sulfur Oxide	2%
Silica	2%
Chloride	0.1%

Classifying these components as either acidic or basic (from a high temperature standpoint), we will end up with two major groups and two elements that we can ignore from an acid-base standpoint. The two that we can ignore are iron and manganese oxides. In the alkaline group of elements are soda, potash, lime and magnesia. The acidic elements are phosphorus, sulfur, and silicon oxides and chloride. Since the chloride is in such a small percentage, we can ignore that too.

Looking at the bare numbers we see that there is much more basic than acidic material present in this ash, with a total of 74% in the four basic oxides. Since each alkaline material must have some neutralizing acidic component in a salt, we have to ask ourselves, how can can this be? The answer is that a lot of the potash, soda lime and magnesia is found as the carbonate (as well as some oxide and hydroxide), since it was fired in an atmosphere containing lots of carbon dioxide, and then existed in the air which contained water vapor and carbon dioxide. Since there is not much sulfate or silicate in the ash, let's turn our attention first to the phosphate. And we must ask, "Is the phosphate present as potassium phosphate, or calcium phosphate, or magnesium phosphate?" And this is really not discernible, because they are all present in the same "sea" of elements. If we had an equilibrated situation, it might be different , but the elements are distributed unevenly in the original wood and the firing has not been high enough to homogenize the ash. Thus the elements are distributed unevenly in the ash and we are no more able to estimate what the soluble salts are than we are able to predict what the percentage composition of any tree's ash is.

The best way to get an idea of how the materials are combined in any given ash is to actually do a separation; to add water to an ash; to allow the ash to settle; to evaporate the wash water to a solid; and then analyze the residue and the washed ash. If for example we find a lot of potassium and phosphate in the evaporate, then we may assume that those elements were combined in the wood ash. On the other hand if we find mainly potassium and hydroxide and carbonate in the evaporate, then we can feel that the phosphate was probably tied up with the calcium or magnesium. It is important for us to realize that calcium phosphate, calcium carbonate and calcium sulfate are rather insoluble. On the other hand, the potassium salts of these compounds are soluble in the concentrations that we are addressing.

We also need to take a look at the glassmaker's use of wood ash to gain some insight into what is happening when we wash ash. The ancient glass makers washed ash to separate the fluxing agents from the coloring agents (iron, titanium and manganese oxides). They wanted to have the potassium and sodium from wood ash without the colorants, so that they could manufacture water white glasses. Therefore, when we wash ash we remove mainly the **alkalies**—potassium and sodium. However, one of the things that the glassmaker found (in using only the product of the washings) was that he got a rather poor glass for his troubles. And the reason for this was that the calcium was left behind with the colorants (since so many of its salts are insoluble) therefore we can expect the same result in our washings. The main thrust of the washing operation is the removal of the sodium and potassium salts without much effect on the calcium, magnesium, iron, manganese and silica.

As far as ash washing and **glaze** making is concerned, there are a couple of good aspects. One is that during the ashing process some of the potassium will be tied up, perhaps as the silicate, so not all of the potassium will be lost. Perhaps 5% of the original potash might remain in the ash residue.

Another good result of ash washing is that the soluble salts will no longer be present to react with the body to give strange looking glazes and bodies. This may be a mixed blessing though, if one of your aims is an **uncommon** looking glaze.

The most useful piece of information that I can give you in this chapter is the result of an analysis of the washed ash, the unwashed ash, and the liquid residue. The following three tables show the results of an x-ray scan of: a) a rather ordinary mixed wood ash without any treatment; b) the same ash after being washed with water; and c) the evaporate from dehydration of the wash water. The results of these analyses are not exact, but since our ashes are so variable in composition and since the washing techniques are variable too, they are entirely appropriate for the samples that we have.

From these x-ray analyses we see that the soluble material removed by washing wood ash is mainly potassium with some sulfate and of course some carbonate.

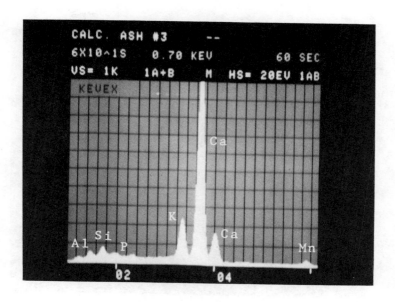

Figure 10.1   EDXR analysis of raw wood ash.

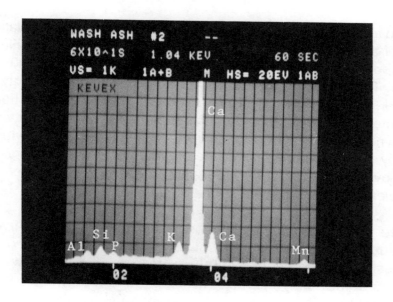

Figure 10.2   EDXR analysis of washed wood ash. Note the
lower potassium peak   height.

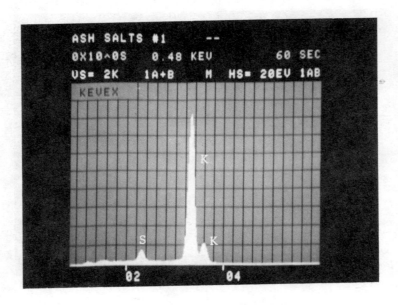

Figure 10.3 EDXR analysis of wood ash solubles. They consist mainly of potassium with some sulfate (carbonates do not register).

In addition to the above information, I did a rough quantitative analysis of the weight of the solubles in a sample of wood ash. First a 500 gram specimen of ash was taken, then it was mixed with 2000 grams of water. This room temperature mix was then stirred thoroughly and allowed to settle. Next a 1000 ml sample of the supernatant liquid was decanted and filtered; and then this supernatant liquid was evaporated to dryness. The weight of dissolved solids was 21 grams. Multiplying this by two (since only half of the original water was evaporated), and then by 0.2 because of the 500 gram sample weight, we see that the solubles amounted to 8.4% of the original ash.

To see if a second washing does much further towards the removal of solubles, an additional 1000 ml sample of water was stirred with the residual slurry and another 1000 ml of supernatant liquid was evaporated to dryness after filtering. This time the residue weighed 5 grams. My conclusion, therefore, is that one thorough washing removes the lion's share of the solubles, especially if a large volume of water is used and if stirring is repeated several times.

Courtesy of Thomas Clarkson

Figure 10.4   Contemporary ash glazed jar.

64

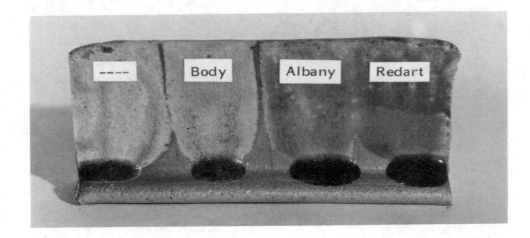

Figure 10.5 Test glazes made with 1:1 mixtures of unwashed wood ash and: no additive; the body composition; Albany slip clay; and Redart clay.

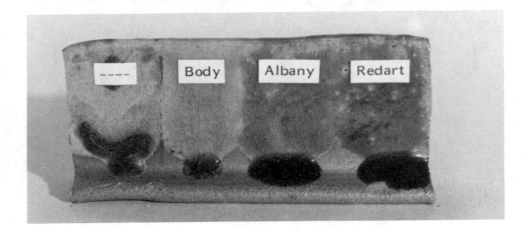

Figure 10.6 Test glazes made with 1:1 mixtures of WASHED wood ash and: no additive; the body composition; Albany slip clay; and Redart clay.

Also, I did run some glaze comparison tests. On sample bars, I ran 4 pairs of glaze tests–with each pair representing one specimen with the original unwashed ash and the other with a washed sample of the same ash. The four tests were 50:50 mixtures of ash with:

1. No additive.
2. The body composition.
3. Albany slip clay.
4. Redart clay.

As can be seen in the photographs of the fired tests, the most remarkable result was that there was **little** difference between pair members. Only on close observation could one see that the unwashed ash glazes were slightly more fluid and slightly more crazed. The glaze colors were just about equal, as were the smoothness or beadiness aspects. The only outstanding difference between pair members was, that in every case, the unwashed ash caused a brown varnish to form on the body below the glaze, while the washed ash did not. So, washing or not washing ash is no big deal!

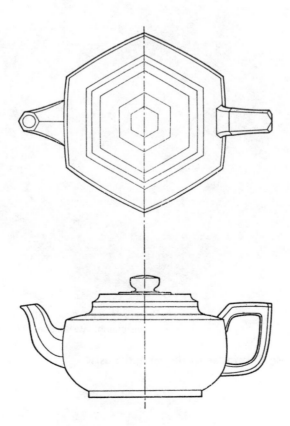

Courtesy of the Freer Gallery of Art, Smithsonian
Institution, Washington, D.C. 20560 (Acq. 49.12).

Figure 11.1 Chinese Chun vase of the Sung dynasty.

11 HIGH ASH CONTENT GLAZES

This chapter will be the most important in the book because high ash glazes are those under consideration when we speak of ash glazes in general. By way of a definition, I would consider a high ash glaze to be one which contains from 30-60% ash. Although one might consider quantities lower than 30% they shouldn't be much less. Also, we shall leave to another chapter those glazes which consist of 100% ash, because that is a slightly different circumstance.

WOOD ASH GLAZES

By specifying WOOD ASH the intent is to deal mainly with ash which is high in alkali. Therefore, it doesn't matter whether it actually came from wood or whether it came from another source and still had the same general composition as wood ash. As long as the ash contains 10-30% potash and 30-60% lime, it can be considered to be a wood ash type. These ashes, in addition to being high in alkaline materials are also low in silica content. Therefore, in working with wood ash glaze formulas we are concerned with additions of silica and alumina to ash. Also, the question arises about what kind of glaze we are trying to make. If we are trying to form a glaze which looks like an ordinary mineral glaze, then that is one thing. On the other hand if we are trying to create a glaze which has an "ASH" look about it, then this is an entirely different subject.

One of the first things to consider about the subject of wood ash glazes is: what is a glaze anyway? Well, primarily, a glaze is a glass, and for most practical purposes, a glass is a silicate. And, being a silicate material, it ordinarily has from 50-80% silica in it. Hence, although we would like to add as much wood ash as possible to a glaze, we have to consider that we need a sizable amount of silica in order to have a "glassy" glaze. There definitely has to be a **sizable** addition of silica to wood ash in a recipe, because there will be little silica in **wood** ash itself.

Another consideration in understanding wood ash is its lime content. Though we recognize that calcium carbonate (whiting) is a flux when it is added to other glaze materials, when it is by itself, it is a very refractory substance. If calcium carbonate is heated to 1000°C it decomposes to calcium oxide. If the oxide is then heated further by itself, a temperature of 2570°C is required before it melts. In fact, if calcium oxide can be protected from the moisture of the air, it makes an excellent refractory. And the same is true of magnesium oxide. The significance of the refractoriness of calcium oxide and magnesium oxide is that if these two materials are present to a large extent in a glaze, they may dominate it and cause the glaze to become refractory and less fluid. Up to a certain concentration these two oxides act as fluxes when in the presence of silica, but beyond a point, they are refractory. Of course another aspect of the alkaline earths is that at certain concentrations of calcium oxide and silica one will find the appropriate concentration for calcium silicate compound formation and items such as calcium silicate and calcium alumino-silicate can crystallize. This has been noted in a number of glazes which give us wollastonite (calcium silicate) and anorthite (calcium alumino silicate) crystals.

ASHY LOOKING GLAZES

To my mind these glazes will have a rough look about them. They will not be smooth and craze-free. However, for them to be acceptable glazes for decoration, we would like them to have a decent durability, so that they don't disappear after one cycle in a dishwasher. For a glaze to have moderate durability one would hope that it would have a 5-10% alumina content and perhaps a 50-60% silica content. If you deal in moles, then you would like to have 0.2-0.3 moles of alumina for every mole of alkaline material, and 2-3 moles of silica for every mole of alkaline material.

The items that will cause a high ash glaze to be distinctive are: a) the soluble alkali salts which penetrate the body and cause reactions and movement of colorants; and b) the high lime content in an ash glaze which will lead to beading of the glaze because of the high surface tension of lime silicates. If we add a rather normal amount of alumina and silica to an ash we may lose the beading property, although the soluble alkali effect will not disappear.

An experiment that I would recommend doing for your own enlightenment, is to take some potassium carbonate or some concentrated ash slurry liquid, and paint a wash of this on the side of a test piece that has a moderate iron content. And, in a position next to this, paint on a **thin** layer of calcium carbonate. Finally, next to that paint a layer of wood ash. Then fire this piece to 1300°C or thereabouts and observe the effect of each of these components on the body. The result for the alkali wash will be a slightly glossy surface with a deeper brown color than the uncoated ware. This is partly the result of the movement of iron in the body and partly the result of the reaction of the potassium salt with the body components to form a sort of glaze—much like a salt glaze. The reaction of the calcium carbonate on the other hand is quite different. It reacts with the body and bleaches it, so that in places where the calcium carbonate is thin you can see a white appearance due to the reaction of the lime with the body and in addition iron decolorization due to the lime. Where the lime has been applied in a thicker layer, the surface will have some dribbles and runs on it because of the calcium aluminosilicate formed by reaction between the lime and the body. It is well known to the brick makers of the world that lime in a brick will cause it to have a paler color than when lime is absent from a high iron brick body. If a final, **very thick** layer of whiting were to be applied, a rough surface would result due to devitrification of high lime compounds. The result on the wood ash glazed section should be a combination of the other two. Some of these results can be seen in the following photograph.

Figure 11.2 A sample plaque fired with washes of potassium carbonate, whiting, and wood ash. Note particularly the dark stain resulting from the potash wash and the dark ring around the wood ash washed area. There is also some slight bleaching to be seen in both the whiting and wood ash coated regions.

HIGH ASH GLAZE COMPOSITIONS

One glaze which I like and which gives a sort of classic "wood ash" effect is a glaze made up of 50% wood ash and 50% Albany slip clay. It has almost all of the traits that I think of as characteristic of an ash glaze, namely: a drippy glaze effect due to the surface tension from the high lime content; a devitrification and crazing where the glaze is thick; a deep green celadon color in thin glazed areas and a brownish tint in thick sections; and a brown, salt glaze effect on the body below the glaze line. A glaze of improved character might be made from this basic recipe by adding 10-20% of kaolin, since the final formula will be a little bit low in both silica and alumina. An example of these glazes is in the following photograph.

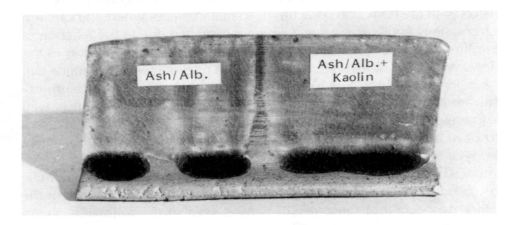

Figure 11.3   A sample plaque fired with a 1:1, wood ash:Albany slip mixture; and with the same plus 10% kaolin. Note the decrease in drippiness after the addition of kaolin.

In general, if ash makes up 50% of a glaze then there will be a strong tendency for the glaze to devitrify (although this may be a desirable trait for your particular project). On the other hand, if a glaze is made up of 40% ash, 40% feldspar, and 20% clay, then the result is a better quality glaze—although it may still be crazed. Such a glaze is shown in the next photograph

Figure 11.4   The addition of 20% kaolin to a 1:1, wood ash:feldspar glaze results in a more viscous glaze with less "ash" quality.

Another way to make an ash glaze is to mix wood ash with the body material—since an ash will form a glaze just by being coated alone on a body. Something in the range of 20-50% ash, with the remainder body, should provide a glaze similar to the one in the last photograph.

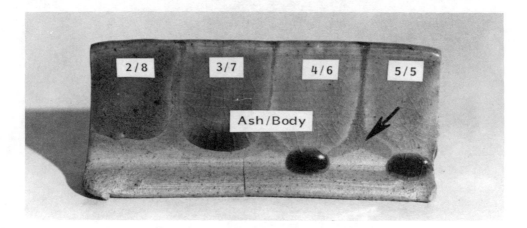

Figure 11.5   The influence of wood ash on fluidity can be seen in this test with varying proportions of wood ash and body material. Also to be noted is the brown body stain at high ash levels (arrow).

Courtesy of Thomas Clarkson

Figure 12.1 Contemporary ash glazed planter

12 GLAZES WITH LOW ASH CONTENT

This should be one of the shortest chapters in this book, because I do not believe in making glazes with low ash contents. The reason I don't, is that a glaze with less than 20% ash content approaches a classical glaze in appearance. Therefore, I don't see much point in trying to replace inexpensive batch materials with a costly, difficult-to-obtain material.

The simple substitution of ash for lime in a glaze, however, makes it an easy task to produce low ash glazes. If you have a particular reason for making low ash glazes (and we are speaking of **wood** ash here), then it is merely a question of taking a normal glaze composition and replacing the whiting with an equivalent amount of wood ash. Because of the differences among wood ashes, you might try adding 10% more wood ash and 10% less wood ash than whiting. As a case in point, consider the following illustration of a glaze in which the whiting has been replaced by ash:

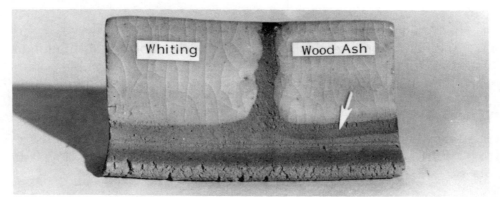

Figure 12.2 A white stoneware glaze: with whiting as a flux; and with wood ash substituted for whiting. The most notable difference is the brown stain surrounding the wood ash containing glaze.

Wood ashes are usually reported to be 30-40-50% calcium oxide, therefore they are very close in composition to whiting which is composed of 56% calcium oxide. The presence in wood ash of other fluxes, such as potash, magnesia and soda, as well as phosphate, will merely accentuate the fluxing ability of the ash as compared to whiting. One exception to my general remarks here is the case of a glaze which is borderline with regard to devitrification or opalization. In a high silica glaze which is ready to opalize, the small amount of phosphate in wood ash can lead to strong opalization. An example of this trait can be seen in the following illustration where a high silica glaze made with lime is compared to the same glaze with wood ash as a flux.

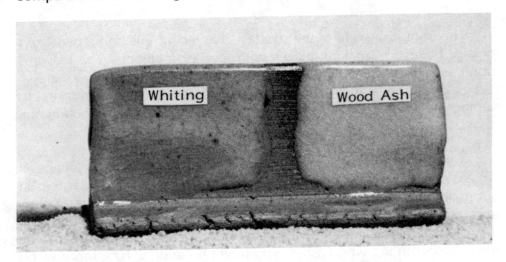

Figure 12.3   A high silica glaze with whiting as the flux (left) and with wood ash substituted for the whiting. The slight phosphorus content of the right hand glaze causes opalization to occur.

Another major glaze difference that is the result of the substitution of wood ash for whiting is the one which occurs because of soluble potash and chloride in wood ash. At high levels of wood ash substitution, this is a large problem, but with 10-20% additions of wood ash, it is not so important. And if one should use a washed wood ash, then the agreement between wood ash and whiting would be even better. An illustration of the bleeding effect due to potassium and chloride in low ash glazes can also be seen in the previous photograph.

One of my favorite wood ash glazes is one that I make up by adding just 20% wood ash to 80% Cedar Heights REDART clay. This clay is commonly used in the Eastern United States, but related clays should not be hard to find in almost any environment, because this clay has a composition almost exactly like that of the average earth's crust analysis. It is just a high iron, siliceous clay whose composition is:

Silica	64%
Alumina	16%
Iron Oxide	7%
Potash	4%
Magnesia	2%
Titania	1%

This glaze can also be made using whiting instead of wood ash and at these 10-20% levels, it is almost impossible to tell the difference between glazes with the two fluxes. This is a very sensitive glaze and illustrates the point that there is not much difference between lime and ash at low levels. An illustration of such glazes can be seen in the following photograph.

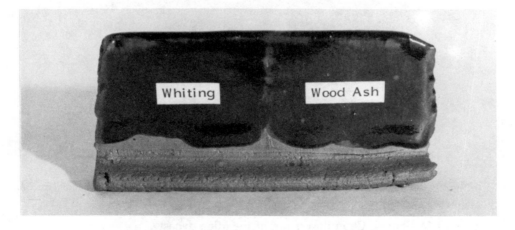

Figure 12.4   Temmoku style glaze with whiting (left) and wood ash (right).

Courtesy of the Percival David Foundation, London (acq. 33).

Figure 13.1 Chinese Chun flower pot of the Ming dynasty.

13 ADDITIVES FOR ASH GLAZES

Although it is possible to add many items to ash glazes, we must ask ourselves: should materials be added to make these glazes look **more** like ash glazes or should materials be added to make them look **less** like ash glazes? I'm for the former, but the latter will also be mentioned.

POSITIVE ADDITIONS

I think, that as practical additives to ash glazes, we should primarily consider those substances which are already in ash. These should be added to our ash glaze batch in order to enhance an effect and make the glaze more ash-like. For example, consider the variability in ash which was discussed in the chapter on ash compositions. The concentration of potassium carbonate in a wood ash may vary from 10-30%; or the lime content may vary from 30-60%. In choosing a specimen we may have obtained a sample which is not representative of an average ash, but is a little low in potassium carbonate for instance. Therefore it seems entirely logical to me to add a dollop of potassium carbonate to the glaze mix in order to have it perform in a way that we would expect for a classical wood ash glaze.

The ability to make appropriate additions, of course, depends on our knowledge of what causes each variation in an ash glaze. For example, we know that potassium carbonate is absorbed by a bisqued body and then reacts in the body to make it more glassy and to make it give up its iron oxide to the surface. If this is an effect that we desire to accentuate, then by all means let us add some more potassium carbonate to the glaze.

We may have discovered that the addition of sodium (or potassium) chloride to a glaze has an interesting effect that we like. We may find that it causes iron to move around and even to be lost because of the volatility of iron chloride. If this reaction is sought, then add a little more sodium chloride to the ash glaze mix.

We have also seen (in the chapter on ash composition) that the action of calcium carbonate in ash is to cause a glaze to have a high surface tension and to bead up in droplets and rivulets. So add calcium carbonate to your glaze if this effect is not noticeable enough in the final product.

However, this sort of thing gets us away from the main topic of this chapter and back into another chapter, the theme of which was: how to make up glaze batches using ash as a component. Well, if we are adding rather ordinary materials—such as calcium carbonate—to our batch then it is sort of a moot question whether calcium carbonate is an ash component or a normal glaze component. And, I don't suppose that it really matters, but in this section let's just stick to items which are found in ash, but which are ordinarily **not** found in glazes. Therefore, the addition of silica or kaolin to ash glazes will not be considered here.

The rather unique parts of ash then, aside from potassium carbonate and potassium chloride, are the phosphate, the sulfate, and the manganese which are present in fairly sizable amounts in most wood ashes. Phosphates can be present in wood ash in amounts of 5-10% so that we can consider adding 5, 10 or even 20% calcium phosphate to a wood ash glaze that we suspect of being low in phosphate for one reason or another. The addition of extra phosphate can have at least three different effects. A dangerous action of phosphates is that in large quantities it can make a non-durable glaze, although I think that we need not worry about this aspect unless the quantities of phosphate are really sizable. The second effect that phosphate can have is to accentuate opalization in a glass or glaze. This is definitely possible in the concentrations that we are talking about. A glaze with a lot of calcium in it and with 5-10% phosphate in it is very likely to form an opal, especially if it is also high in silica. A third influence of phosphates in glazes is that of lowering the melting temperature, but this is not something that is predictable, because it depends very much on the other constituents in the glaze. Some phosphates (such as aluminum phosphate) are actually very hard to melt, while some phosphate glasses are quite low melting.

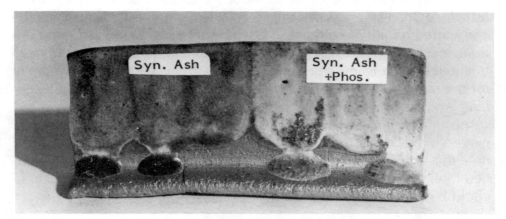

Figure 13.2 A comparison of a synthetic ash wash with (right) and without added phosphate. A 10% addition of calcium phosphate causes strong opalization of the glaze.

The sulfate in wood ash is rather a unique component, but I am not quite sure whether it is desirable in a glaze. There is one outcome that I think might be useful, and that is the tendency of sodium or potassium sulfate to form an immiscible liquid which can float on top of a glaze. It is quite possible that this could form streaks on the surface of a glaze. However, whether one would desire this situation or not is problematical. Sulfates are rather hated materials in glass-making, where they often form a scum on glass surfaces.

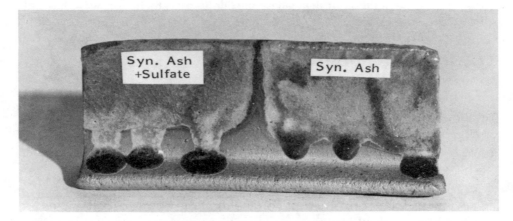

Figure 13.3 A comparison of a synthetic ash wash with (left) and without added sulfate. A 5% addition of potassium sulfate has little effect on the ash glaze.

Finally, let us consider the result of the addition of manganese to an ash glaze. Manganese is certainly a colorant, but in ash glazes it can be considered a natural colorant. If a whole series of wood ash compositions in Wolff's work is examined, we see that frequently there are large quantities of manganese present in wood ash. In fact it is not infrequent for the manganese oxide content to be higher than the iron oxide content. And, as noted in the chapter on coloring agents in ashes, we can suspect that whenever there is a brownish cast in an ash glaze that manganese is the cause. Therefore, if we start off with an ash glaze batch and note that it gives a rather pure celadon color, and if a brownish, devitrified look should be desired in the glaze, then some form of manganese could be added to get this result.

Figure 13.4 The addition of manganese dioxide to a synthetic ash wash has little effect.

COLORANTS AS ADDITIVES

This section might also be entitled: "gilding the lily." An ash glaze is rather a coarse, rough-looking glaze with earthy colors due to iron and manganese. Therefore, if we add such a thing as cobalt oxide, we may have a color which pleases us, but whether it any longer looks like an "ash" glaze is questionable.

As far as I am concerned, if you feel that the colors of ash glazes are not bright enough, then go to another type of glaze—don't try to make ash glazes colorful. They are not basically bright glazes. They are soft, subtle glazes that are appropriate only for certain sizes, shapes and kinds of vessels with suitable bodies. From an aesthetic point of view, I normally wouldn't try to make a **colorful** ash glaze. And whether one should use ash glazes on delicate porcelain ware is very problematical.

You could add cobalt to an ash glaze if you desire, but try 1/4% or less—no more than is absolutely necessary. Or, try combinations of cobalt with iron and/or manganese to tone down its "blueness." The same goes for chromium oxide or copper oxide. Always consider the peculiar charm of ash glazes before altering them.

If I were going to add coloring agents to ash glazes I would limit myself to three items. They would be, in order of preference: iron oxide (especially in reduction to get celadon-like colors); manganese oxide at fairly high concentrations (2-5%) to get good browns and to get devitrification; and finally, a little titania might be all right. One thinks of titania as a common impurity of earthy materials, because it certainly is a contaminant of our clays and the earth around us. It doesn't happen to be present in very high quantities in wood ash, but it would be a reasonable addition in low amounts because of its earthy qualities and its influence on the color of celadons. Any large additions of titania would lead to matte glazes though.

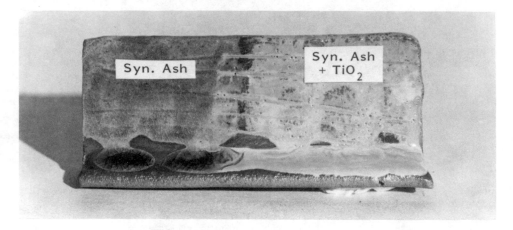

Figure 13.5   The addition of 10% titania to a synthetic ash results in an opaque white glaze (right).

Courtesy of Thomas Clarkson.

Figure 14.1   Contemporary ash glazed plate.

14 LOW MELTING ASH GLAZES

The first comment that should be made about low temperature ash glazes is that this is sort of a contradiction of terms, because the first ash glazes were definitely high temperature affairs. They amounted to either the reaction of ash with a ceramic body, or the blending of an ash with ceramic body raw materials and the application of that blend to a piece of ware.

However, for those who would like to fire at temperatures below cone 8, it certainly is possible to make glazes with ash that will melt at least down to cone 04 (about 1050°C or 2000°F), and yet still have the quality of an ash glaze. However one needs to be very aware of the composition of wood ash before it is used in experiments. If you look down a long list of the compositions of various wood ashes, the impression you would get is that ordinary wood ash is very high in lime and moderately high in potash, magnesia and phosphate. My impression after looking at such a list would be that the calcium oxide content of an ordinary wood ash might be 25-50%; the alkali content might be 10-30%; the magnesia content might be from 5-10%; and the phosphate content might be around 10%.

With these numbers in mind, we might then consider a technique for making a low firing glaze. Naturally, the first thing that comes to mind is the use of a frit. Since our ash already contains a large amount of lime, it would be logical to try a frit which has no lime content at all. One such frit is #25 frit from Pemco, or its equivalent #3189 frit from Ferro. Still another frit which might be promising is #3185 frit from Ferro which is merely a sodium boro-silicate frit. This #3185 frit, with wood ash, plus some clay to supply alumina, might be very practical. Naturally in a low temperature glaze, the content of wood ash should not be excessive. A 20-25% content of wood ash might be the maximum reasonable amount to use in a low temperature glaze because of the possibility that high ash quantities with higher calcium content would lead to devitrification.

FRIT COMPOSITIONS

	Pemco #25	Ferro #3185
Potash	5.4%	–
Soda	14.7%	7.7%
Lime	0.5%	–
Zinc Oxide	0.7%	–
Alumina	12.1%	–
Boric oxide	16.9%	38.2%
Silica	49.7%	54.1%
Fluoride	1.8%	–

In brief trials with both of the above frits I did obtain glazes, and in the case of #25 frit, a pale green celadon appeared—although it was highly crazed and somewhat devitrified. However, the "ash" quality of both glazes was minimal, because the percentage of ash that could be added was low.

The two simple frit glazes that I used were:

GLAZE ONE

3185 Frit	- 65%
Wood Ash	- 25%
Ga. Kao.	- 10%

This produced a mottled, pale white glaze at a temperature of about 1200°C. It did not have any "ash" characteristics.

The second glaze was:

GLAZE TWO

#25 Frit (or 3189)	80%
Wood Ash	20%

This gives a fluid, semi-matte celadon glaze when fired to about 1200°C and it was highly crazed on the particular body I was using. When the second glaze was underfired, it gave some very rough-looking glazes that might be usable, but it appeared to be a very temperature sensitive glaze. These two glazes may be seen in the photograph.

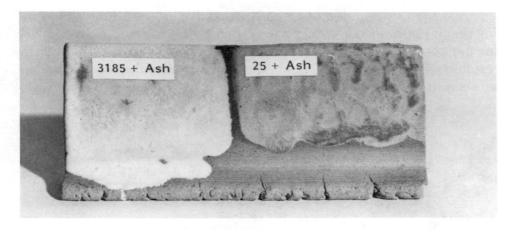

Figure 14.2   Two low-fired fritted glazes with ash.

Perhaps the most practical way to make a low fired glaze would be to take an ordinary, known recipe from a reliable source and then substitute wood ash for one of the fluxes in the recipe. For example, Nelson gives a formula for a cone 04 colemanite crackle glaze which calls for:

100 Potash Feldspar
123 Colemanite
 43 Barium Carbonate
 33 Flint

By substituting wood ash for the barium carbonate, one might expect an acceptable glaze to result. When I tried this substitution the glaze melted well and in fact was quite fluid. In appearance it was a fine, opaque milk white opal. However, that was the trouble! It looked like an ordinary opal glaze and had no "ash" quality at all.

Another glaze, offered by Rhodes, is a cone 04 colemanite barium matte and this calls for:

47 Feldspar
10 Flint
11 Colemanite
13 Whiting
13 Barium Carbonate
 4 Zinc Oxide

A straight substitution of 15 parts wood ash for the 13 parts of whiting ought to produce a good glaze. When I tried substituting wood ash for the combined whiting and barium carbonate, a matte white glaze resulted which was not very fluid. The appearance of the two glazes can be seen in the next photograph.

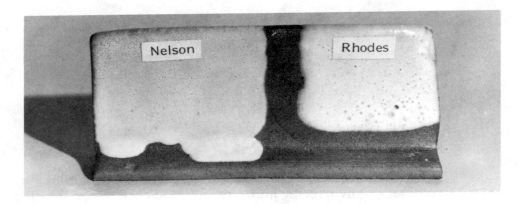

Figure 14.3   Two low-fired glazes made with ash.

My only advice to someone desiring a glaze at still lower temperatures is: try it, it might work!

15 SYNTHETIC ASH GLAZES

Anyone who has made ash glazes, and has gone through all that that implies must have given a thought to the possibility of making synthetic ash. To form ash by burning some raw material, to collect ash, and wash it, and to worry about possible contamination, and then to try to reproduce a good ash glaze, has to have impressed upon one the desirability of finding a simpler way of operating. Furthermore, if you have any consciousness at all of the present world, you will realize that there are substitutes available for almost every inanimate thing we encounter. Natural rubber has been replaced to a large extent by the synthetic; natural fibers have been replaced by Dacron, Orlon and Nylon; the siding on houses is either aluminum or vinyl; wood panelling is found to be plastic coated fiberboard—hardly anything is what it appears. Naturally these materials do not duplicate the originals 100%, but they could, if we wanted to go to enough trouble.

Therefore we have to ask ourselves, "can we make a synthetic wood ash (or any other ash) that would very closely duplicate the real item?" If it were a problem of making a material that looked like wood ash in the raw state, namely a fine powder with the appropriate color and particle distribution, then we might indeed find that it would be hard to make an exact replica. However, the ash that we put in our glazes is almost completely altered during the firing process, so that the fineness of the powder may be of little consequence once an ash has been completely combined in a glassy form. As an indication, the following photograph shows a glaze made up with both ground and unground natural ash. There is little difference between the two compositions.

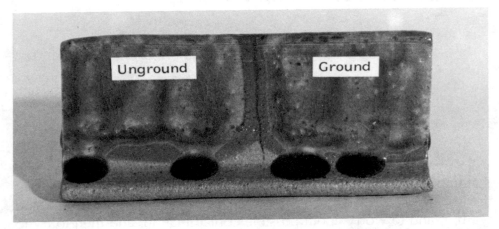

Figure 15.1 Two glazes on a sample plaque, one containing ground ash and the other one unground ash. There is little difference between the glazes.

Another characteristic of ash that is sometimes irritating, but which operates in our favor as far as synthesis is concerned, is the variability of ash. No two ashes act the same, therefore, who can say that an imitation ash that we might make is not the exact duplicate of some "unknown" ash.

Frankly, I believe in the practicality of making synthetic ashes. In fact I am strongly in favor of making synthetic ashes. I believe that someone who voluntarily uses a natural ash has to be a bit of a masochist.

As an example of what I mean, consider the natural wood ash that I have used in most of my tests. I got this ash by a very simple technique. I have a neighbor who heats his house during the winter with wood, and thereby generates an enormous quantity of wood ash. I just went to his house, and asked him if he would be willing to part with a few pounds of this material. And, he was extremely happy to be of help when I explained my need. He is not a gardener, therefore he had a problem with where to dump it. [The amusing part is that our local trash pickup will not accept ash (for a very good reason, namely, that they never know when a hot coal might be buried in the ash and when they dump this in with combustibles they could have an instant "fire" truck)]. Thus ash can be a problem.

In any event, my neighbor gave me a large sack full of ash, I thanked him profusely, promised him a bowl (which I never delivered) and then, with this large sample of ash went through all of my experiments.

While this was very simple for me, I actually have no idea what combination of tree wood went into the making of that ash. Furthermore, I don't know whether the wood that he used was treated gently before he burned it. I know by looking at his wood pile that he used tree trunk sections with the bark on, but I am unaware of how far those trees were dragged over muddy ground, and whether a lot of dirt was captured in the bark. This was a suitable ash as far as I was concerned because it made good looking ash glazes and gave me a uniform product to conduct a great number of tests. Still, the background of the ash had some doubts in it. And this is almost bound to be the case, unless you heat your own home with wood and are always careful to wash off the bark. Even then, can you be sure that all of the trees were grown on good soil or poor, wet lands or dry, in sunshine or shade? Unless you are willing to devote your whole life to the accumulation of the "perfect" ash, you are going to end up with one kind of compromise or another.

As a final excuse, let me say that I am basically a chemist at heart, and I always have a strong feeling that anything that occurs naturally can be closely reproduced by a thoughtful chemist. We can duplicate almost exactly the chemical composition of many materials and with a little effort we do very well in duplicating the physical condition of a material. So I feel that with relatively accurate analysis figures, such as can be obtained from Wolff's book, we can take natural minerals and by using fine particle sizes and the appropriate chemical combinations we can come very close to duplicating an "average" ash.

EXPERIMENTAL

A sample was made up using selected raw materials with the aim of duplicating the type of ash which would be formed by burning beech wood—as noted in an analysis of the ash from a beech tree trunk from Wolff's book. His data showed the composition of one beech wood ash to be that given in formula I. However, (and this drove me up the wall) there was another analysis of beech tree trunk ash later in the book and it furnished the numbers in formula II. What a shock! We certainly don't have to worry much about decimal points when such variations occur naturally.

	I	II
Silica	1.5%	0.8%
Lime	63.4%	41.6%
Magnesia	11.3%	19.6%
Soda	2.9%	2.2%
Potash	15.8%	26.5%
Phosphate	2.7%	5.7%
Sulfur Trioxide	1.5%	0.9%
Chloride	0.1%	—
Iron Oxide	1.0%	1.3%

A batch was made up to give approximately the percentages found in formula I. It was:

    52.1 grams Dolomite
    77.5 grams Limestone
     2.5 grams Calcium Sulfate
     5.9 grams Bone Ash
     1.5 grams Minusil-5 Silica
     0.2 grams Sodium Chloride
    23.2 grams Potassium Carbonate
     1.0 grams Ferric Oxide
     4.8 grams Sodium Carbonate

Obviously, if there are differences in nature as great as those between formulas I & II, then it would be perfectly legitimate to make up a formula as approximate as this:

    50 grams Dolomite
    75 grams Limestone
     3 grams Calcium Sulfate
     6 grams Bone Ash
     2 grams Minusil-5 Silica
    0.2 grams Sodium Chloride
    25 grams Potassium Carbonate
     1 grams Ferric Oxide
     5 grams Sodium Carbonate

And furthermore, since some of Wolff's beech tree ash analyses contain 1-10% manganese oxide, it would all right to add a couple of percent of powdered manganese oxide if a little deeper color were desired.

All of the materials in the synthetic batch were either in a fine powder form or were ground to such a condition using a mortar and pestle. The batch was then mixed by thoroughly shaking the powders in a jar. For the calcined ash portion, the mixed powder was placed in a sagger and the sagger was fired in a slow kiln to approximately 650°C. This temperature was not high enough to remove the carbon dioxide from either the calcium carbonate or the potassium carbonate, hence in my synthetic mixture there was a sizable amount of soluble material, (mainly the potassium carbonate). If one wanted to make the equivalent of a washed ash, the potassium carbonate could be eliminated and a **small** amount of a potash feldspar could be substituted.

The two glazes that were made up and placed on the sample plaque were 1/2 ash (either fired or unfired) and 1/2 Albany slip clay, mixed and painted on the surface of the test plaque. The plaque was then fired to 1300°C in a reducing atmosphere. The results may be seen in the following photograph. It is apparent that there is little difference between fired and unfired synthetic ash.

Figure 15.2   Two glazes made from equal parts of Albany slip clay and either natural wood ash or synthetic ash. There is little difference between the two glazes.

After the above tests with synthetic ash, a further test was made to compare the synthetic ash with natural ash. The fired version of the synthetic ash was painted on 1/2 of a test plaque, then my standard wood ash was painted on the other half of the test plaque. This plaque also was fired to 1300°C in a reducing atmosphere and showed very little difference between the natural ash and the synthetic ash, as can be seen in the following photograph.

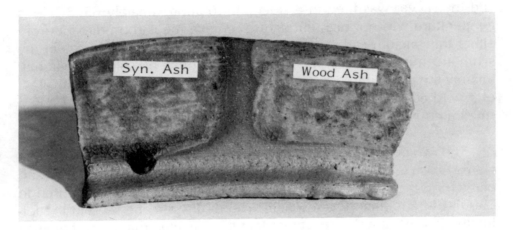

Figure 15.3   Washes of both synthetic ash and natural ash were painted on a plaque and were fired to 1300°C. There was little difference between the two final glazes.

If the preceding synthetic wood ash seems too complicated, then try the following mixture, which contains the essential ingredients for a simple synthetic ash:

25 Limestone
25 Dolomite
12 Pearl Ash
5 Bone Ash
1 Iron Oxide

Still another experiment was run in which three test plaques were made with three ordinary glazes. On each plaque a single glaze was first made with calcium carbonate as the major flux, next, on the same plaque, the glaze was made with synthetic wood ash as the flux, and finally the glaze was made with common wood ash as the flux.

The glaze on plaque one was a simple 80% feldspar-20% flux glaze. On plaque two, the glaze was made up of 4 parts feldspar, 3 parts of silica and 2 parts of flux. The third plaque was the same as number two plus one part of kaolin.

After firing the plaques to 1300°C, the most obvious effect was the similarity of the glazes on each plaque. The glazes on plaque one were all crazed and fairly clear (though bubbly); the glazes on plaque two were all opalescent because of the high silica content; and the glazes on plaque three were intermediate in appearance. While there was some small difference in fluidity due to the different fluxes, one can imagine that this could be adjusted by varying the flux contents slightly. Because of the similarities on each plaque, we can believe that natural and synthetic wood ash are equivalent in effect.

In fact, any "ash" may be duplicated in this way. A synthetic straw-type ash was also compounded and it performed excellently when used to make a replica of a Chinese Chi-chou bowl.

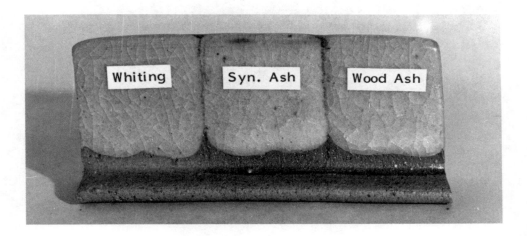

Figure 15.4   Glaze number one was made using 4 parts of feldspar and one part of flux. The three fluxes are identified on the plaque.

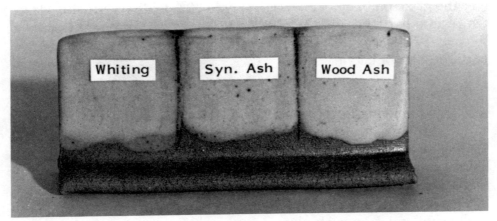

Figure 15.5 Glaze number two was made using 4 parts of feldspar, 3 parts of silica and two parts of flux. The three fluxes are identified on the plaque.

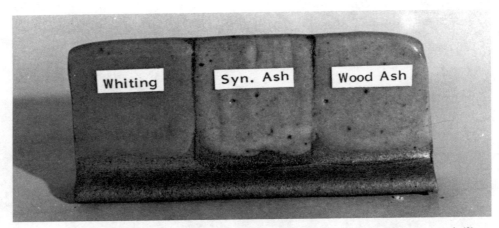

Figure 15.6 Glaze number three was made using 4 parts of feldspar, 3 parts of silica, one part of kaolin, and two parts of flux.The fluxes are identified on the plaque.

Summarizing, these tests have shown the feasibility of making a synthetic material which is perfectly acceptable as a substitute for natural wood ash.

16 FAKE ASH GLAZES

Samuel Azzaro, in his master's thesis at Alfred University, gave three glaze formulas for what he called "fake" ash glazes. He remarked that these formulas had the characteristics of ash glazes without containing ash. The formulas will be given here because they are excellent examples of the type.

I.	60	Albany Slip Clay
	30	Whiting
	10	Barium Carbonate
II.	64	Albany Slip Clay
	16	Edgar Plastic Kaolin
	20	Whiting
III.	50	Albany Slip Clay
	20	Whiting
	20	Barium Carbonate
	10	Flint

Mr. Azzaro specified that the glazes were to be fired at cone 9-10, and he remarked that they gave either runs or beads on their surface.

When I made up sample glazes with these compositions, the results were as shown in the first figure. Formula III had the best drips and runs, but formula II had the best "ashy" color. A compromise might consist of formula III with a percent or two of added manganese oxide to muddy up the color a little.

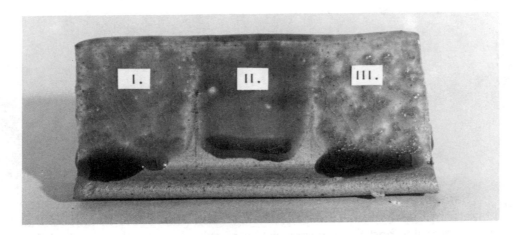

Figure 16.1 Examples of tests made using Azzaro's glazes as given in the text. Example 3 was the drippiest glaze.

All of these glazes are of the type that we would anticipate might give an "ashy" appearance, knowing that many wood ashes contain high amounts of alkaline carbonates and other alkaline materials. So we would expect a glaze with an excessive amount of such material in it to give us a drippy, runny glaze. In this regard, we may consider some of the following as possibilities: besides the Albany slip clay that Sam Azzaro recommends, we could also make up glazes with Redart clay, ordinary glacial shale (or brick clay), or Barnard clay (if we wish a dark glaze). In each of these cases we could take about half base clay and add to that either half whiting or a mixture of whiting with other bases.

The second illustration shows a sample plaque with some glazes of this type.

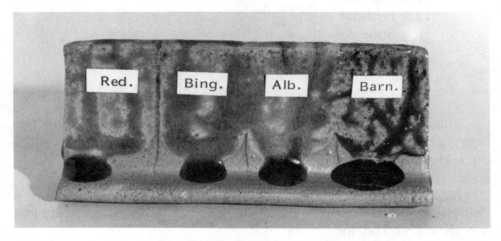

Figure 16.2 Examples of simple glazes made up with 1/2 whiting and 1/2 clay (Redart; Binghamton brick clay; Albany slip clay; Barnard slip clay). Barnard slip clay and whiting gives a nice runny brown glaze.

In addition to Mr. Azzaro, Grebanier also makes remarks about "synthetic" wood ash, and his recipes with this component could also be considered to be "fake" ash glazes (with no disrespect intended). The batch recipe that Grebanier made up for a synthetic pine ash was:

44.4% Whiting
36.2% Feldspar
 4.1% Bone Ash
 6.4% Magnesium Carbonate
 4.4% Soda Ash
 2.3% Manganese Dioxide
 2.3% Iron Oxide

Sanders also gives a formula for a synthetic ash. This one was recommended by Maritaro Onishi, it is:

62% Limestone
12% Feldspar
 7% Bone Ash
 5% Magnesite
10% Kaolin
 3% Silica

The only notable missing elements in the latter are iron and manganese, and they may have been supplied in the original recipe by either the feldspar or the kaolin.

Basically then, a fake ash glaze might consist of about 50% of a "dirty" clay (rather low in alumina) and about 50% of a flux mixture that is high in lime content.

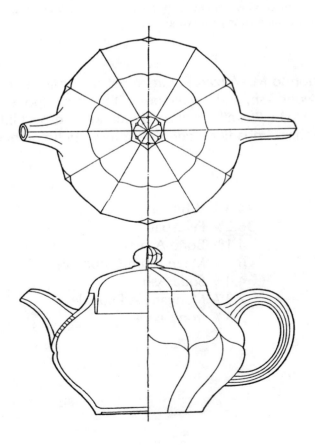

17 CEMENT AS AN ASH SUBSTITUTE

It is not often that we are able to find an inexpensive and useful material to use as a glaze component when ash-like glazes are desired, but Portland cement (not concrete) is such a material.

Portland cement is a high-fired raw material made from substances such as crude limestone and raw clays. The mixed minerals are fired to temperatures near 1500°C to generate a "clinker," and then this mass is ground to a fine powder. If it were not for the fact that cement has a relatively low silica content, the process would have produced a glass. Even so, it does have a glassy aspect because there is some silica and alumina in it.

A nominal composition for cement is:

Lime	62.5%
Alumina	7.5%
Silica	22.5%

These numbers add up to a total of only 92.5%, but this is because there are small percentages of other elements present. For example, in an average Portland cement there is: a percent or two of iron oxide, a couple of percent of magnesium oxide, a percent of sulfur trioxide, some alkali, and a percent or two of volatiles (water and carbon dioxide). These are all quite variable though, and are not too important for our calculations, so we can use the above numbers for rough computations. The similarity of the percentage of lime in cement (62.5%) to the percentage in limestone (56%) and to the percentage of alkalinity in an average wood ash (66%) means that one-for-one substitutions (cement for whiting) are reasonable for cement use in many glaze formulations.

Converted to moles, the above figures yield:

$$1.00 \text{ CaO} : 0.07 \text{ Al}_2\text{O}_3 : 0.34 \text{ SiO}_2.$$

If we compare this composition to an ash, say of a tree trunk, we see that the principal missing element is potassium, which is usually found in a fairly high percentage in wood ash, but which contributes less than one percent to the constitution of Portland cement

The high lime content of cement, even though it is in a combined form, causes it to be an inconvenient material for normal glaze formulation, because it is so basic (caustic) in nature. This, however, is not too different from the effect that we note with a natural wood ash. To get rid of this problem it would probably be desirable to have a cement which had been exposed to the atmosphere for some days or weeks. Unfortunately when cement is exposed to the atmosphere in bulk it will tend to harden to a rock-like material. This means that through aging we would lose one of the benefits of cement, namely its floury nature. Normally cement is available as a powder, the majority of which will pass through a 200 mesh screen. For this reason, it is a practical material for glaze making. Whether it is a more desirable material than calcium carbonate is for you to answer. But if you like ash, then you should also admire cement.

The iron contamination in cement should be fairly uniform because it has been well mixed before calcining. One would expect that a cement-containing glaze would make a fairly uniform celadon. We have tested this theory and have found that a glaze made up of 20% cement and 80% feldspar with no other additives will make a transparent green celadon on a porcelain body. The shade of the celadon will probably vary according to how much titanium and manganese are present in the cement, but in our test, the color of the glaze was very uniform in areas of the same glaze thickness.

When similar tests were made, using either wood ash or limestone in place of cement, the resulting glazes were both identical, pale, baby blue celadons. This result indicates to me that there was practically no titanium in the wood ash, but that there must have been a percent or so in the cement. Note the appearance of the glazes in the following photograph.

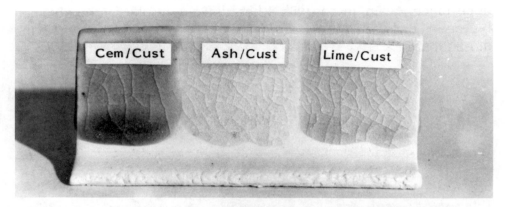

Figure 17.1   Three glazes made with 4 parts Custer feldspar and one part of flux. The fluxes were: cement; wood ash; and whiting. The cement containing glaze was a dirty celadon with noticeably less crazing than the others.

It is possible to make a glaze from cement using the same practice as was used with ashes, namely by using cement as a direct substitute for whiting (limestone) in formulations. As noted before, one could take twenty percent cement and add it to eighty percent feldspar to make a glaze. However, this will give a glaze which is a little bit high in alkalies and a bit low in silica, therefore, if some kaolin were added, a better glaze would be obtained, as can be seen in the next illustration.

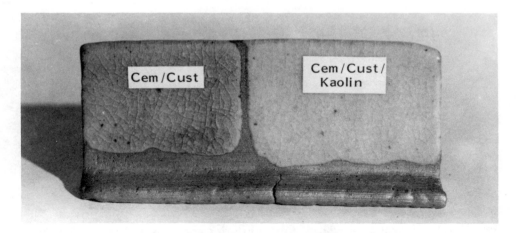

Figure 17.2   The addition of 15% kaolin to a 4/1 feldspar/cement glaze improves the crazing and leads to a translucent glaze because of trapped bubbles.

It is also feasible to use cement as a wash or slip much as you would use ash. One can make up a slip of finely ground cement and either spray, dust or drip it on an unglazed pot to obtain a rather rough glazed appearance. Again, just as with ashes, different results can be obtained by varying the wash thickness from thick to thin. This can be seen in the illustrations.

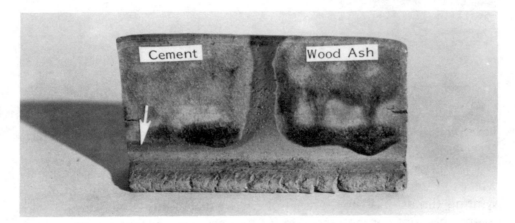

Figure 17.3   A cement wash glaze does not differ greatly from a wood ash wash glaze and even has a brown stain at the base (arrow).

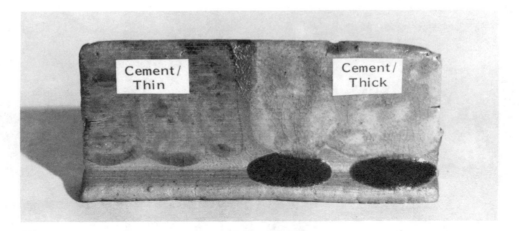

Figure 17.4   Cement wash glazes also form drips and runs and in addition give bleached areas when the thickness is appropriate.

18 IDENTIFICATION OF ASH

Brother Daniel has a very good section in his book on practical identification methods for ashes. I would like to comment on his material and then expand it a little bit.

Since the exact chemical analysis of a complex material such as ash takes many man-hours to accomplish and may also require the use of several exotic instruments, it would be very expensive to get a good analysis of any ash. However, there are some things that can help us. In the first place, almost everything on this earth has already been analyzed at one time or another, as we can see in Wolff's opus on ash analyses. Thus, if we know what has been burned to give the ash that we have, then we can get a good idea of its composition by looking in Wolff's work. Since all natural materials have sizable variations in make-up, such an estimate may be just as good as an analysis.

There are times though, when we have an ash sample about which we have general but not specific information. For example, we may have wood ash which comes from a householder's furnace. We know that it is wood ash but neither of us may be aware of whether it is mostly oak, ash or pine ash. Also, if we should happen to generate ash by burning discarded hay, then we definitely have a mixture of plant ashes. In the latter case we wouldn't know whether it came primarily from grasses, crucifers, or papilionaceous materials. Nevertheless, there are some general observations that we can make about ash which will help us use it more effectively in our glazes.

ANALYSIS BY SUBSTITUTION

As an aside from Brother Daniel's work let me submit a technique that I recommend for evaluating wood ash.

The main question with regard to our ash is: do we have a high lime and potash content alone, or do we also have a lot of silica present?

First of all there are some simple tests available. We can take the ash, add water to it and test the water for alkalinity. If we have a material which is high in potassium carbonate and calcium hydroxide, then the result will be a slurry which either gives us a strong blue color when tested with litmus paper, or which feels slippery to the skin (although one should be careful not to get too much on your fingers). This is not extremely valuable though, because almost any ash has a certain amount of alkaline material in it and even a small quantity of alkali carbonate will give a strongly basic reaction.

I think that the best test, therefore, is a straight substitution in a glaze formula. We all have favorite glazes, so if one takes a favorite glaze formulation and substitutes an ash for whiting in the glaze, then it can be observed whether the substitution was an equivalent or not. For example, I have a favorite 4-3-2-1 glaze (feldspar-silica-whiting-kaolin). If this glaze is made up with wood ash substituted for the whiting, we can then compare two glazes and see if the ash acts like pure whiting or not.

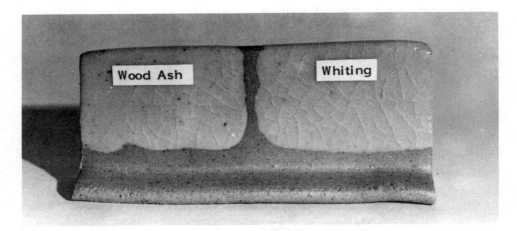

Figure 18.1   The 4-3-2-1 glazes made with either whiting or wood ash at the 2 level are quite similar in appearance. In fact, they are almost identical.

Teapot – 9" height, thrown and altered, with textural slip, ash glaze and oxides. (By Thomas Clarkson)

Platter – 15" diameter, with textural slip, ash glaze and oxides. (By Thomas Clarkson)

Large footed bowl – 21" diameter,
thrown and altered, with textural
slip surface, ash glaze and oxides.
(By Thomas Clarkson)

Covered vessel – 16" height, thrown and altered, with textural slip, ash glaze and oxides. (By Thomas Clarkson)

Covered vessel – 14" height, thrown and altered, with textural slip, ash glaze and oxides. (By Thomas Clarkson)

Covered vessel – 16"
height, thrown and
altered, with textural
slip, ash glaze and oxides.
(By Thomas Clarkson)

Teapot – 10" height, thrown and altered, with ash glaze and oxides. (By Thomas Clarkson)

Platter – 15" diameter,
textural slip, ash glaze
and oxides. (By Thomas
Clarkson)

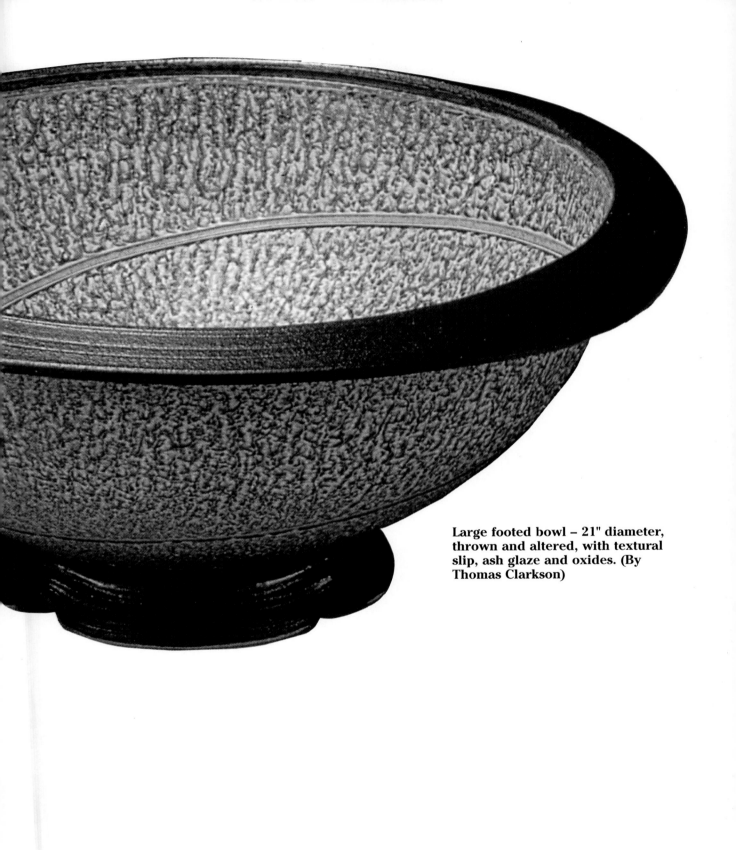

Large footed bowl – 21" diameter,
thrown and altered, with textural
slip, ash glaze and oxides. (By
Thomas Clarkson)

Large vessel – 24" height,
thrown and altered, with
slip, ash glaze and oxides.
(By Thomas Clarkson)

Bowl with handles – 14" diameter,
thrown and altered, with textural
slip, ash glaze and oxides. (By
Thomas Clarkson)

Oval bowl – 15" long, thrown and altered, with hand built additions, ash glaze and oxides. (By Thomas Clarkson)

Covered oval vessel – 16" long, thrown and altered, with hand built additions, plus ash glaze and oxides. (By Thomas Clarkson)

Jar with oval lid – 12" height, thrown and altered, with hand built lid, ash glaze and oxides. (By Thomas Clarkson)

Vase – 15" height, thrown and altered, with slip, ash glaze and oxides. (By Thomas Clarkson)

Jar with oval lid – 12"
height, wheel thrown and
altered, with hand built lid,
plus ash glaze and oxides.
(By Thomas Clarkson)

This may seem like a rough test, but it is not really so bad. And it certainly is better than paying a hundred dollars for an analytical test whose quality will also be unknown.

As far as soluble alkali is concerned, we can learn something about this question by making a glaze test on an iron-containing (1-2%) body with the same ash substituted glaze as above. If in this case we see a brown "flashing" occurring at the unglazed bottom of the ware, we can suspect that there is a large amount of alkali in the ash. This not a positive proof, but it does give us another hint. To test the effect, make up a concentrated slurry of wood ash and paint a bisqued test piece with just the liquid from the slurry. The flashing produced is partly due to the anions (negative ions) such as chloride and sulfate and carbonate, and partly due to the alkalies, because the two are found together.

Another test would be: to substitute the ash for other constituents in the 4-3-2-1 glaze. For example, a high silica straw ash might be found to be a good substitute for feldspar. In another test, the straw ash might substitute for the silica . . . and so forth. However, there would be no point in substituting ash for clay, because ashes have almost no alumina in them.

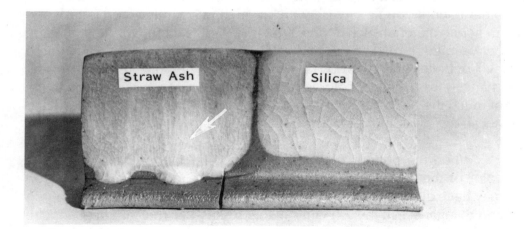

Figure 18.2   When straw ash is substituted for silica at the 3 level in a 4-3-2-1 glaze it has two major effects. First it makes the glaze more fluid and second it causes some opalization (arrow) because of its phosphate content.

Brother Daniel mentions that a method for classifying an ash is by measuring the weight of ash produced by calcining. In the case of ash from wood, one usually finds that the ash content is less than 1.5% of the original wood weight. On the other hand, a straw ash may amount to as much as 5-8% of the original material. All of the high percentage ashes are found to have high silica contents. However, this information may not be too valuable, because if we were able to weigh the original material, then we would have been able to identify it by category and could look up this class in Wolff's compendium.

A much more practical technique used by Brother Daniel is that of employing a calcining test to determine the nature of the ash. He makes tablets out of ash samples by pressing them very hard in a wooden mold. A pellet can also be made from wood ash and a cornstarch slurry—add boiling water to cornstarch, then make a paste of ash and a minimal amount of this liquid. Interestingly enough, wood ash pellets are hard to form by pressing because the powderiness of this ash does not lend itself to cohesion. On the other hand, straw ash will form a sturdy pellet due to the "stringiness" of the ash. Brother Daniel recommends firing the test tablets to 900-950°C on an inert plaque (perhaps silica). At this temperature one would lose carbon dioxide from calcium carbonate, thus if you have an ash which is high in whiting, it will change into calcium oxide (lime or quicklime) during the firing. On the other hand if you fire an ash which is high in both lime and potash and an acidic material such as silica, then at 950°C there will be a reaction between these oxide types and you will get a glassy result. When I fired two buttons, one of wood ash and another of straw ash, the former changed from a khaki colored friable tablet to a grey-green friable tablet of much the same size. The straw ash pellet on the other hand fused and became a hard, grey-to-black frothy mass that was fused to the tray.

When the buttons of wood ash first come out of the furnace, the color of the ash that was due to carbon from incomplete combustion may have disappeared. On the other hand the color which is due to iron and manganese in the ash will still be present and you can draw conclusions from that. Brother Daniel recommends that the samples then be placed in a humid atmosphere, after which they can be checked for moisture absorption. Those samples high in alkali absorb a lot of water and the high silica samples do not.

Figure 18.3 Pellets of wood ash (left) and straw ash (right) react differently when fired to 950°C. The straw ash pellet has fused to a dark glassy mass while the wood ash pellet remains friable and will eventually absorb moisture and carbon dioxide from the air and disintegrate.

The color in a fired ash sample can be deceiving though. The color that is found in a crystalline mineral (such as the unsintered ash) can be quite different from the color in a glass, especially if the oxidation state is not known. Moreover, the colors from iron and manganese (the main colorants in ash) can both be brown, or can be a variety of hues, depending on the matrix, the firing atmosphere, and the substrate. About the only sure opinion one can draw is; if the ash is snow white there is not much iron or manganese present; while on the other hand, if the fired ash button or bead is a dark brown, then either iron or manganese or both are present.

An underglaze streak test can be run to see if anything further can be found about iron and manganese in ashes. Mark a bisqued porcelain plate with a fused ash sample, and fire the plate in both a glazed and an unglazed state to see if a color develops. Then compare the results with streaks of materials known to contain either iron or manganese or both.

A quicker version of the firing test can be run using a propane torch (such as is used by plumbers), but be sure to use eye protection during the test. The ash tablets can be placed on a soft brick and then be heated gently in the propane flame until they are glowing. If the button is hard and fused, then it was a grass-type ash (with a high silica content). While if it remains powdery and unfused, then it probably was a wood ash.

Brother Daniel has another interesting observation with regard to the fusibility of ash and that is a comparison of the ash to the original form of the material. For example, if you fire a sliver of wood, it curls up and readily turns to a pile of powder. On the other hand, if you fire a stalk of straw, it maintains its basic shape because the alkaline and siliceous materials have fused and have formed a delicate replica of the original structure. This doesn't help us too much though, because to run the test we obviously have to know what it was that we originally fired.

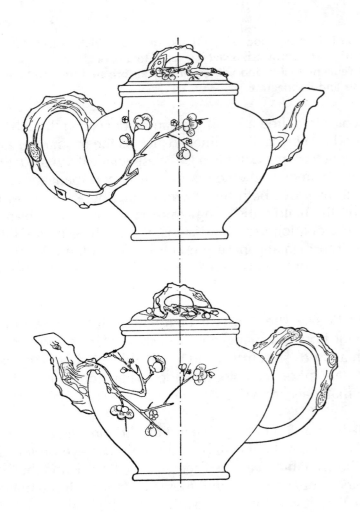

19 ASH ONLY GLAZES

These glazes will give us what can be considered to be classical ash effects on ceramics. The result will vary, from a thin varnish-like glaze; to a runny, drippy glaze; to a dark, rough devitrified glaze.

SOLUBLES AS GLAZES

If one rinses a wood ash with just enough water to extract the solubles from the ash and have them in a fairly concentrated form, then you will have the material that was sought by the ancient **glass** makers. This liquid will contain the fluxing elements so valuable for the glass manufacturer. Actually the things extracted are materials such as potassium, sodium, carbonate, chloride, phosphate and sulfate ions. If one wanted to make 100 grams of an artificial mix, one might try adding one gram of sodium chloride to ninety-nine grams of potassium carbonate as a first approximation, with perhaps added pinches of potassium phosphate and sulfate.

If this solution is sprayed on a ceramic (preferably a stoneware) in a rather light coat, then the net result after firing to about cone 8 will be a varnish effect—a light gloss on the surface of the piece. If too much of this liquid is sprayed on, then the body may slump or deform, because the liquid penetrates the body completely and not only fluxes the surface, but also fluxes the interior, which is not desirable.

Figure 19.1 Varnish-like glazes made by painting ash solubles and potassium carbonate on a stoneware body. Both glazes are extremely glossy.

The result of firing this liquid on the ceramic will be a finish that has a relationship to some of the early Japanese ware. If you have a ceramic which has a uniform and high (2-3%) iron content, then the varnish will be a nice nut-brown color, though this will vary according to how the iron is dispersed in the body. The effect is much like that which one would obtain on the first firing of a new salt kiln, when only a light salt finish appears on the ware.

STRAW ASH GLAZES

Since straw ash contains both reasonable amounts of silica and reasonable amounts of alkaline materials, it may be considered to be a glaze in itself. And if a straw ash is slurried with water, ground finely, and then applied to a body, the result will be a glaze with no further additions needed. Again, this glaze should probably be applied only in thin layers, because there will be some solubles in it also . Since the ash from straw does not contain much alumina, if one wants a smooth glaze, then a thin glaze is best, because in this way the ash will be able to extract alumina from the body. If thick layers of straw ash are applied, then running will occur because of the lack of alumina in the ash itself. Other than that the glaze will also pick up iron from the body (if this is available), and one can expect celadons to result after reduction firing.

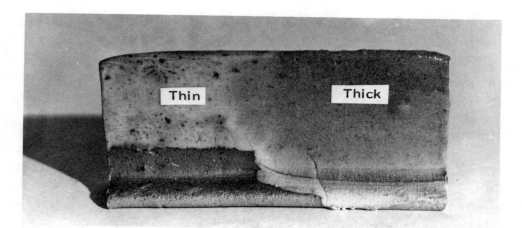

Figure 19.2 Straw ash slips applied to a stoneware body in thin and thick layers. The thin layer is slightly opalescent, while the thick layer is clear. The thick layered region is similar in color to the grey Korean Koryo celadons.

WOOD ASH ALONE

A finely ground slip made up only of wood ash and water, will be, to my mind, the most effective way to treat a ceramic with ash in an effort to obtain a **unique** glaze. A thin application of such a slip will produce everything which is fine about ash as far as glazing is concerned. In the first place, the solubles will be absorbed by the body and then will diffuse to the surface on the application of heat. Thereupon they will give a varnish effect near the base and in places where the glaze runs thin. Next the calcium and magnesium in the slip (present in high concentrations), will react strongly with the body material, furnishing alumina and silica and iron to the glaze, to give a nice celadon appearance in reduction. Finally, the high alkaline earth content will cause a high surface tension and will give the unique, drippy, crawly glaze which is the classical wood ash effect. Another minor result from this application of the ash alone, will be body bleaching, which is variable, depending on the thickness of the ash application.

If you want one glaze to succeed when using ash, an ash slurry application is the one that I would recommend. This, in combination with a good throwable body, will provide an exceptional glaze that will give character to your work. It is sort of a "poor man's" salt glaze since it allows you to operate without corroding your kiln (although you must recognize the fact that the volatility of the halides in wood ash will certainly have **some** effect on your kiln).

Courtesy of Thomas Clarkson.

Figure 20.1   Contemporary ash glazed bowl.

20 SALT WASHES

One of the unique effects in ash glazing is the absorption by the ceramic body of soluble salts from the ash mixture (slurry). These salts do not dissolve in the body, but are absorbed through a wicking effect, and initially move from the salt solution into the body pores.

Let's take a close look now at a possible mechanism for what happens. In the first instance we'll use a glaze which is only a mixture of ash and water. The mixture will be a slurry which is part solution and part solid suspended in solution. The solids will of course consist of insoluble materials of the ash, such as silica, calcium phosphate, calcium carbonate, etc. The solubles, which will be present in the ash-water mixture are items like potassium carbonate, sodium carbonate, sodium and potassium chlorides, sodium and potassium sulfates, and perhaps some potassium phosphate.

REACTIONS

After applying the solution-slurry to the outside of a bisqued bowl, the solids will remain on the exterior, and some of the liquid will be absorbed by the body. The liquid, of course, is a solution and is not merely water. Once the solution has moved into the body, a number of things can happen. If we had a raw body there would undoubtedly be some ion-exchange between the potassium ions and sodium ions of the solution and the hydrogen ions of the clay, to form compounds of a complex type. In a bisqued body, however, there will not be much of this type of reaction because the clay will have been transformed during the bisquing operation into precursors of mullite and the exchange capacity will be greatly reduced. Therefore, on drying this ash-glazed body, the water will evaporate and salts will precipitate, both in the body and on the surface of the body. There is a great tendency for the salts to move to the surface during this air-drying operation. [This is the same type of effect that one sees when one is making slip-cast ware in plaster molds. There the soluble salts move through the plaster body and precipitate on the outside of the plaster mold when it is dried. On plaster these salts are probably materials such as sodium sulfate and sodium carbonate.] This particular movement of the soluble salts to the surface of the ware is a solution movement and is implemented by concentration gradients, where the moisture is moving to the outside of the piece (where it evaporates), with the salt following the moisture.

There is another type of movement however, and although it is similar in net result, it is quite a different effect and should be considered separately. An explanation will be attempted in the next paragraph.

If the ceramic piece is placed in a kiln and is slowly brought to the reaction temperature of the salts, then some further actions will occur. One of the first things that will happen will be a melting of the low fusing salts. For example, sodium chloride will fuse, since its melting point is around 800°C. This molten salt can either combine with the body or it can move by surface flow in the body pores. Another action that will take place will be the reaction of the most corrosive salts present in the body. As an illustration, potassium carbonate, which is extremely corrosive at temperatures of several hundred degrees Celsius will be actively reacting with some of the body constituents. A reaction to be expected is that of sodium or potassium carbonate with finely divided silica to form alkali silicates. And at only slightly higher temperatures they will react with alumina from the clay to form aluminates. We could term this action a glassification process where these alkalies are performing as fluxes. At higher temperatures, a salt such as sodium chloride will also react with the body though in a slightly different way. It will give glassy products and will free chloride ion. This is similar to the process in salt glazing where sodium chloride decomposes into its ions (and/or atoms) and then forms glassy sodium silicates, sodium aluminosilicates and hydrogen chloride.

There are other aspects of this operation in the high temperature region which we should now consider and they are volatility and fluidity of the materials in the body and the glaze. This is particularly important in regard to iron oxide and iron chloride. The presence of chloride ions and iron contamination in the body means that the two can react together to form iron chloride which is both low melting (315°C) and volatile. In any case, iron moves to the surface of the body. If, instead of using a salt glaze, we merely dip a bisqued body into a salt solution and then fire it, it will be found that the surface has a much higher concentration of iron in it (as noted by its color), than the interior of the body. The iron has reacted in some way with the halogen and then moved to the surface, where it has collected to form a high iron oxide surface on either the body or the glaze or both. A photograph taken of a body cross section will show this. This particular photo was taken of the cross-section of a 2% iron containing body which had been dipped in a salt solution and fired to cone 8-10. The iron has obviously moved to the surface.

Figure 20.2 Body-glaze cross section showing body region (arrow) depleted in iron. Though not too apparent in cross section, the amount of iron that has moved into the glaze can readily be seen in the darkened area on the outside.

For an even more noticeable reaction of this type there is the case of copper. Copper, as the chloride, is extremely volatile and will move completely out of the body and glaze and will be swept out of the kiln. Obviously there are many reactions going on in our kilns, and there will be other contaminants in the body and glaze (such as manganese, titania, and vanadium), that can be moved appreciably because of the volatility of their chlorides.

SALT WASH GLAZES

A fascinating experiment to perform is one in which various salts in solution are painted on the sides of a specimen whose body contains about 2-3% iron oxide. For example, from such an experiment one can learn about the volatility or the movability of the compounds in the body itself. Here we can see the difference between the volatility of iron chloride and iron phosphate. If we paint the specimen with a solution of sodium phosphate (such as one might get in a washing compound), or paint on this same piece some sodium chloride or potassium chloride, then one can see this effect: The sodium phosphate painted portion remains relatively light in color (though quite glossy), but the portion of the bowl painted with the sodium chloride solution becomes a much deeper brown than the original color. An intermediate color will be formed when something like a sodium sulfate solution is painted on a plaque.

Figure 20.3 Stoneware plaque with sections painted with various solutions: borax; sodium phosphate; soda ash; and sodium chloride. All areas were glossy except for the borax region.

All of this should be expected, because a look at a chemical handbook will show that iron chloride is quite volatile, while many other iron salts are either not volatile, or they decompose to form the oxide. For example iron sulfate will decompose at moderate temperatures to give iron oxide and an oxide of sulfur. These compounds would not be as prone to move the iron around as is iron chloride, which moves as a molecule and transfers the iron easily from one place to another. This is well known to salt glazers who make extensive use of iron as a colorant in their glazing operations.

Incidentally, it may not be a good idea to do a great deal of glazing of this type outside of saggers, because the volatile components will wreak havoc on kiln refractories, thermocouple tubes, oxygen sensors, etc.

Figure 20.4   Interior of a wood fired "dragon" kiln in Yi-hsing, China. On the ceiling, frozen drips can be seen where the wood ash has reacted with the refractories.

On looking at the effects of these tests, one can't help but be impressed with some of the results. For example, painting the body with sodium phosphate solution gives one a very glossy, smooth surface which SEEMS to be quite desirable. However, before being carried away by this technique, one might do well to test the durability of the glaze formed in this fashion, because phosphate glasses are notorious for being slightly soluble in water. I remember taking a bowl glazed in this fashion, putting it in a dishwasher and being disappointed at the outcome. Enough leaching occurred to give an iridescent surface to the glaze. So the results are not as fabulous as they seem at first sight. The final result will be very dependent on the maximum temperature, kiln dwell time, and the type of salt used. You can get some good iron colors, though, and I have obtained some promising results both with plain bodies and with iron slipped bodies.

A note of CAUTION. One must be careful to have the salt-washed bodies **extremely** dry before placing them in a kiln. For example, I had a sodium chloride soaked body EXPLODE in a kiln, because it was just slightly damp.

Another possibility is to avoid the intermediate steps and take materials like iron chloride, iron sulfate, etc. and use them as stains on the bodies. It is possible to simply paint decorations on bodies, using iron chloride in water solution as the paint, just as one could use a soluble salt of cobalt. The only advantage that this might have over a slip is that it could allow painting of finer lines and more delicate shades.

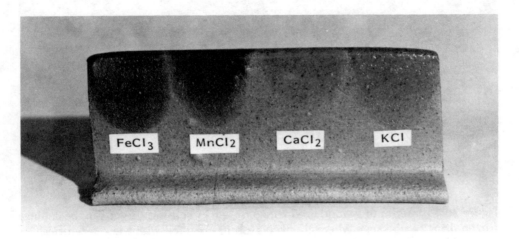

Figure 20.5   Brown stains result when iron chloride and manganese chloride solutions are painted on a stoneware body.

An example of iron and manganese chlorides fired on bodies can be seen in the above illustration.

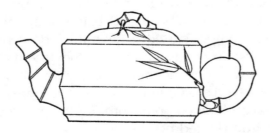

21 GLAZE THICKNESS & APPLICATION

A typical ash glaze is fairly thin when applied, although thick in areas of beading. And, while an ash glaze should not be as thin as a salt glaze or a modern porcelain glaze, it is still at its finest when applied rather sparingly.

The final glaze thickness may be a bit deceptive though, because it is difficult to judge it from the amount of raw glaze that has been placed on an article. This is because the glaze (if it is a typical one of about 50% ash), reacts strongly with the body, and therefore the glaze thickness will be due, not only to the applied glaze, but also to the glaze generated by the reaction of the applied layer with the body. In this way an ash glaze is similar to a salt glaze, where sodium from the sodium chloride reacts with the clay, feldspar and silica of the body to form a glaze. In an ash glaze the alkali carbonates and the alkaline earth carbonates decompose to alkali and alkaline earth oxides and then react with the silica, feldspar and clay of the body to form a glaze.

EXPERIMENTAL

A worthwhile experiment to perform is to take an ordinary ash glaze of either 100% ash or perhaps 50% ash and 50% Albany slip clay and apply this to a test piece in several different thicknesses. In this way an optimum glaze thickness can be discovered. A variation of this test is to inscribe marks on the body so that an estimate of the filling capacity of the glaze can be judged also. One merely has to take a rasp-like tool and score the body in places where the several glaze thicknesses will be applied. An example of some tests can be seen in the next photograph.

Figure 21.1   Glazes resulting from painting 1,2,3,4 or 5 layers of wood ash slip on a stoneware body. Once a minimum thickness has been achieved, then dripping and body bleaching will occur.

Observation of the finished article in the photograph, shows that with an extremely thin glaze layer the appearance of the surface is rather dry and bumpy. And this is normally not desirable. A slightly thicker glaze layer will give the appearance which we usually associate with ash glazes. In this case it will be runny and there will be teardrops coursing down the side of the vessel like rain running down a window pane. On the other hand, if too thick a layer is applied, then we can again get a dry appearance and occasionally a darker color. The dry appearance in the latter case is due to the fact that ash is refractory. We like to think of materials such as lime and potash as fluxes, yet in excess they are refractory.

In a glaze of the correct thickness, we note, in our experiment, some of the characteristics of ash glazes: the first is a glossy darkening on the body near the outer edge of the glaze-body interface due to the movement of the potassium carbonate and other salts through the bisqued body; the second characteristic is the rather light colored areas in the glaze where the body has been bleached and approaches a white color; and a third feature is the beady nature of the glaze due to the elevated surface tension of high lime glazes. Whenever we see these effects on a ceramic body, we can suspect that the piece was glazed using a recipe with a considerable percentage of ash.

GLAZE APPLICATION

The appearance of a wood ash glaze will depend to a certain extent on the coarseness of the particle size of the ash. However, for this particular section, let's consider only a very finely ground wood ash, either by itself, or mixed with material like Albany slip clay. Such a uniform glaze could be applied by spraying, by dipping, by painting, or by slip trailing.

For a good control of thickness, the glaze coating technique to be preferred is spraying, especially since the thickness of the glaze is very important for the final appearance. Using an air brush or a spray gun, the glaze can either be applied very smoothly or it can be coated non-uniformly by varying the time and distance of spraying. One advantage of using a spraying procedure for applying an ash glaze is that the deposit can be made to resemble the natural fall of ash in a wood fired kiln. However, one must be careful in using this technique, because it can look quite phoney if overdone. In fact, one suspects that some of the Japanese glazes which have an "ashy" look about them have been applied by a spraying technique, to give this appearance. There are not many places in a wood fired kiln where a good natural ash deposit can be counted upon to give a glaze. It is much easier to give a "natural" ash fall appearance to a glaze by spraying it on and then putting the piece in a place in the kiln where the ash doesn't reach.

All other techniques for applying ash glazes to ware are truly secondary to the spraying process, except perhaps for slip trailing. In this case, a pseudo-runny effect can be achieved with slip trailing in an effort to represent the effect of the natural running of an ash glaze, but again, this technique is very easy to overdo, and it should be used with restraint.

A good procedure to use for applying ash glazes to ware, might be the use of a combination of techniques. One could dip the upper part of a vase or pot in an ash glaze, and then work out the border between the bare body and the glaze using either a spraying or a slip trailing technique.

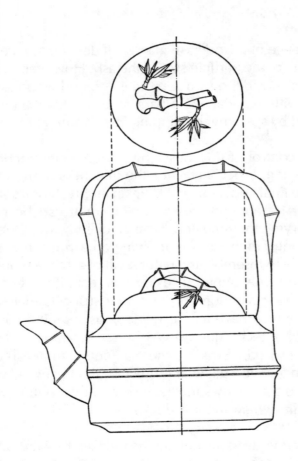

22   ASH-BODY INTERACTIONS

Although the body has a pronounced influence on most glazes, it has an especially important effect with ash-only glazes. This is due to the fact that to get an **ash** result we frequently have to use a thin layer, so there is more reaction (percentage-wise) of the body with the ash than would be the case if the glaze were thicker. In addition, ash-only glazes are rather fluid, and with their movement over the body they tend to pick up more of the body constituents. And finally, one more outcome is that ash-only glazes are quite corrosive because of their high lime and potash content. This leads to an increased reaction of the ash with the body when compared to the reaction of an ordinary stoneware glaze.

One of the first things to consider is: how much difference is found between applying an ash glaze to a raw or green body versus applying an ash glaze to a bisqued body? My problem is that I am prejudiced in favor of bisqued bodies. This is because my experience has been that applying a glaze to a raw body leads to more glaze defects than applying a glaze to a bisqued body. I have read accounts in the literature which state that all one needs to do is to get **used** to glazing on raw bodies, and, that once you get used to it there is not much of a problem. This may be, but I have never gotten **used** to the technique. Nevertheless, one factor to consider is the probability that the Japanese and the Chinese always applied their ash glazes to an unbisqued body. Therefore, if you really want to reproduce an oriental glaze (even as far as including the same defects), you should seriously consider applying ash glazes to a raw body. However, my feeling along this line is that by varying the bisque temperature you can arrive at a fired body with a porosity and reactivity that is comparable to a raw body.

Figure 22.1 Picture of an ash glaze (1:1, wood ash:Albany slip) fired on a raw body and on a bisqued body. On the raw body some non-wetted areas can be seen.

The major action that occurs when applying an ash-only glaze to a ceramic body is the absorption by the body of the liquid from the ash slip. And, if you have used an unwashed ash, the ash glaze slip will be very alkaline, and this alkaline liquid will penetrate the body whether it is raw or bisqued. If too much of this alkaline liquid penetrates the body, it will have a definite effect on the hardness of the body. Hence it is quite possible to derange the body firing temperature enough so that distortion and slumping will occur after firing the ash glaze. This is especially true for thin articles. For larger pieces with thick walls, this may never be a problem, although there is the possibility that expansion differences may occur which can weaken the body. The liquid will be high in potassium and sodium salts and these alkalies will then cause the body expansion to increase wherever they are present permanently. I use the word "permanently" with malice aforethought because it is rather difficult to tell what happens to all of the liquid after it is absorbed by the body. One cannot be too sure where the alkali has settled out, i.e., whether it has penetrated the body completely and been distributed uniformly, or whether it has only penetrated part way and has given us an expansion gradient because of this.

Still another influence is due to the fact that alkali ions migrate readily and tend to collect on surfaces. This can be noted if you dip a bisqued bowl in salt water and then allow it to dry. The salt moves to the surface. This is undoubtedly related to surface tension differences, capillarity effects and many other complex physical factors; and I really don't have the answer to it. All I know is that there is an effect. We can either make use of the effect or we can be overwhelmed by it. One way that it can be used was explained in the chapter on salt glazes, where bowls were painted with salt water to get a thin varnish-like layer.

Connected with this action of the ash solubles on the body is the influence of the body on the ash. While this may not be literally true, it appears that the body alters the kind of glaze that we get. If we consider that a pure ash glaze consists primarily of calcium oxide (which would almost be true if we were using pure wood ash), then we have to consider the high temperature reaction of calcium oxide with the body. The body normally will have sizable amounts of silica and clay and feldspar in it as major constituents, and titania and iron as minor constituents. The lime will react with this silica, feldspar and clay at high temperatures. The beauty of the result will be the ability of these reactants to form glasses, and this requires a sizable amount of silica in the end product, namely from 50-70% for practical glazes. Since a mixture of wood ash with feldspar, clay and silica makes a good glaze batch, then the reaction of plain wood ash with the body also makes an acceptable glaze. Because high fired ceramic bodies are high in alumina and silica, it is to be expected that the reaction of a high lime wood ash with the body will produce a fairly good glaze as far as durability is concerned. However, if the reaction is not allowed to go to completion, but occurs in a fairly short period of time, the final glaze may contain a lot more lime than would normally be present in a good high-fired glaze. This high lime content produces a glaze which has a high surface tension and this is why we notice the beading effect on these high ash (or high lime) glazes.

If your desire is to get a smooth glaze, without a running and dripping effect, then the aim should be to lower the lime content by one technique or another. Normally this would be done by adding material to the ash (such as feldspar, clay and silica) before it is placed on the body, thus ensuring a better reaction between the lime and the glaze-forming ingredients. But, when concerned with a 100% ash glaze, the lowering of the lime content of the final glaze must be arrived at by using a **thin** glaze. When we put a thick ash layer on a body the reaction

Courtesy of Thomas Clarkson

Figure 22.2   Contemporary ash glazed covered jar.

is not complete, because of viscosity problems and penetration problems. Nevertheless, to me, the most desirable characteristic of ash glazes is the drippy, dribbly runniness of the whole scene. So, why try to avoid it when it gives desirable character to the glaze.

As noted before, it is stoneware bodies that seem most appropriate as bases for ash glazes. And since stonewares have reasonable amounts of iron (1-3%), it is to be expected that the iron will be part of the material that moves into the glaze as the ash attacks the body. Thus it is common to obtain celadons when firing in reduction, or yellowish glazes when firing in oxidation. The titania content of the body will also influence the celadon coloration. The less titania, the bluer, and the more titania, the greener the celadon will be.

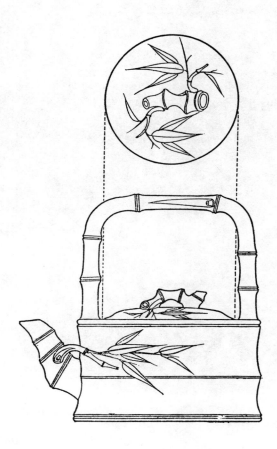

Courtesy of the Nelson-Atkins Museum of Art,
Kansas City, Missouri.
Purchase: Nelson Trust (31-136/1)

**Figure 23.1 Chinese Ceramic Jar,
1st Century B.C., with ash glaze (height 15").**

23 FIRING ASH

One of the observations made by Brother Daniel was that it is difficult to make a judgement on the composition of ash by its color. The reasoning behind this is that frequently carbonaceous materials are left in the ash after firing, and these dark materials will mask the presence of iron and manganese, which are the most common coloring oxides in ash.

One technique that can be used to remove the carbonaceous coloring materials in ash is to refire it in an oxidizing atmosphere to a temperature which will cause the carbon to burn off completely. This is not an easy temperature to estimate however, because of the possibility that carbon may be present either in a coarse or a finely divided form. Also, it may be mixed more or less intimately with the inorganic materials in the ash. Ideally, 600°C would be a reasonable temperature to use for the removal of carbon. However, if temperatures above this point are used, then problems with volatility and fusion may occur.

These same difficulties also will be found because of the temperature at which the ash was originally fired, and this can vary over quite a range depending on whether the original organic material was burned briskly or was burned slowly; whether it was burned in the open with a breeze blowing on it; or whether it was burned in an enclosed furnace with very little air circulation (such as the condition we find in some of the newer iron stoves which are built to allow slow, long term burning of wood).

The crux of this chapter, however, is not merely how carbon can be removed, but also what the effects are of varying temperatures on the quality of ash with regard to its usefulness in glazes.

WOOD ASHES

Under this heading will be considered all of the ashes which are basic in nature and which have relatively low silica contents (mainly wood ash, but also some hay ash). If we thought of an idealized wood ash which contained only potassium and calcium salts, such as the oxides and the carbonates, then it wouldn't be too difficult to predict what might happen on firing. Potassium salts will only give up their water and carbonate contents at relatively high temperatures. In fact it will be quite difficult to remove carbon dioxide from potassium carbonate using only thermal means. With calcium compounds, the situation is different. It is still hard to remove water, but the carbon dioxide from calcium carbonate will be removed at temperatures above 900°C. In fact, if one takes pure limestone rock, and fires it in the open to temperatures over 900°C, the end result will be a soft powder consisting principally of calcium oxide. However the real world is not like this and in all wood ashes—even those that are primarily basic—there are some acidic materials. These would consist of a small amount of silica and a modest amount of phosphorus pentoxide. Because of these acidic components there will be some mineral formation or actual glass formation and this will make clinkers. There will be some melting and incipient fusion and adhesion between particles. And, depending on the amount of acid in the batch, there may even be formation of a true clinker.

With regard to volatility, the chlorides are the chief culprits. For example, iron chloride and alkali chlorides are relatively volatile at firing temperatures, and because of this volatility we may experience not only the loss of the chloride—which might have a desirable effect in our wood ash—but also the loss of cations such as iron and titanium or potassium and sodium.

If, for whatever reason, one refires a wood ash, it is advisable to keep the top temperature within reasonable limits.

There is another problem also, and that is the increase in water absorption for the elements in wood ash if they are fired to a high temperature (about 1000°C). There will be loss of carbon dioxide and water on firing to high temperatures, and on cooling, the material (unless protected from the air) will pick up moisture and carbon dioxide. Brother Daniel illustrated this well by making up pellets of wood ash, firing them, and then allowing them to stand in the atmosphere for several days. We have duplicated this experiment and it is illustrated in the accompanying photograph, where samples of wood ash have been made into pellets and then fired to high temperatures. This illustration demonstrates the disintegration of fired pellets after standing in the atmosphere.

Figure 23.2   On the right of the photograph is a wood ash pellet immediately after firing, and on the left is a fired wood ash pellet after standing several days in a humid atmosphere. The left hand pellet has changed back to the hydrated carbonate.

STRAW ASH

Although the title of this section is STRAW ash, it is meant to include all ashes which have a fairly high content of silica. This content of silica causes a reaction to take place when high temperature firing of the ash occurs. In other words, the alkaline materials in the ash will react with the silica to form silicate glasses or minerals just as they would in a body or a glaze. In fact some of the high silica ashes may be considered to be self-contained glazes (as can be seen in the illustration).

Figure 23.3 A stoneware plaque with a pure straw ash glaze and a pure wood ash glaze. The wood ash has reacted with the body to form a glaze, but the straw ash is a glaze in itself.

Thus, if one is trying to remove carbon from straw ash, it may be very difficult to do this without causing the ash to form a clinker or without causing the ash to become glassy.

Since the presence of carbon in an ash is not all that terrible, it should not worry us a great deal. It just causes the minor inconvenience of our not being able to estimate whether there is much iron or manganese in the ash.

FIRING TEMPERATURE AND WASHABILITY OF ASH

If one happens to be of the group that finds it desirable to wash ash before using it in a glaze, then it certainly behooves you to have a reproducible firing history for your ash. If you have a high alkali ash, and are counting on washing to remove all of the alkali, it won't be much of a problem. But if you have a high silica ash, and you do not wish the alkali to be present in the final ash product, then it is certainly very important not to fire the ash to a high enough temperature to react the alkalies and alkaline earths with the siliceous material or other acidic material in the ash. In the case of a high fired ash, the reaction of the acidic and basic materials can certainly form silicates which are not readily soluble in wash water. A description of this was given by Brother Daniel, who gives a percentage composition of an ash, which—although high in alkaline material before washing—was still high in alkaline material after washing, because it had originally been heated to a high temperature and hence the alkaline silicates were rendered inert to washing.

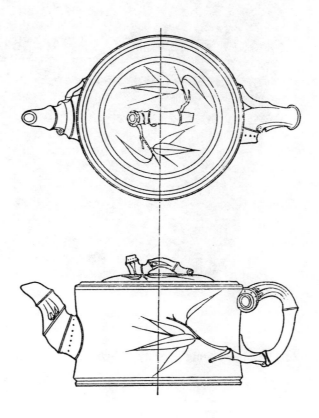

Courtesy of the Freer Gallery of Art, Smithsonian
Institution, Washington, D.C. 20560 (Acq. 10.3).

Figure 24.1   Chinese Sung dynasty Chi-chou bottle with mottled glaze.

24 DECORATING WITH ASH

CHI-CHOU WARE

The classic use of ash as a decoration (as opposed to its use as a simple glaze) stems from the so-called Chi-chou ware of south central China. Along the Kan River, about 150 miles south of Nanchang, in the province of Kiangsi, is a small village called Yung Ho, with a heritage of making a type of temmoku ware. During the Sung dynasty (960-1279 AD) this Chi-chou ware was made from a dirty white body which was covered with a deep brown glaze, ornamented with a cream-to-yellow overglaze decoration. The fame of the Chi-chou ware is based not so much on the beauty of the glazes involved, as on the skill of the decorators using the technique.

Based on experimental tests, the light colored overglaze decoration apparently was made from a straw-type ash. Since this ware originated in south central China, the straw may have come from rice or a wild plant. A similar decoration can be made using wheat or oat straw ash, but it doesn't have quite the same color or fluidity. My best replicas came from a synthetic reed ash with the following composition:

> 60 Pearl Ash (Potassium Carbonate)
> 40 Minusil-5 (Silica Flour)
> 20 Dolomite
> 20 Bone Ash
> 10 Potassium Chloride
> 4 Iron Oxide
> 4 Manganese Oxide

Courtesy of the Freer Gallery of Art, Smithsonian
Institution, Washington, D.C. 20560 (Acq. 13.38).

Figure 24.2   Chinese Sung dynasty Chi-chou bowl with cut paper design.

The Chinese used at least three different techniques for applying this straw ash to the base glaze. One of the most notable of the decorations made use of cut paper designs either in the form of positive or negative paper cuttings. It is possible to cut paper so that either the paper represents the desired design, or the holes in the paper represent the design. Both of these procedures were used by the Chinese. The wet paper was probably stuck to the unfired dark brown glaze and then the straw ash slurry was either spattered, sprayed, or hand dotted over and around the paper. Then the paper was removed and the article was fired, with the end result being a picturesque design in pale yellow or cream over a dark brown ground. It may not be "fine" art, but it is good folk art.

Courtesy of the Freer Gallery of Art, Smithsonian
Institution, Washington, D.C. 20560 (Acq. 13.40).

Figure 24.3   Chinese Sung dynasty Chi-chou bowl with mottled glaze.

A second means of applying the glaze was simply to dot it on in appropriate patterns, probably using a fine tipped brush. In this way a more freely applied decoration would result. Often the straw ash would be applied in large blobs and then if the glaze was overfired the decorations would run and mottle and give a very pleasant streaked effect, sort of mindful of an inverse leopard pattern. This type of decoration requires a little restraint and a great deal of knowledge on how the firing is progressing. If the glaze is underfired there is too much of a straw ash presence and a roughness will occur. On the other hand if there is overfiring, then the entire glaze can end up at the bottom of the vessel. As with all ceramics, the size and the shape of the article have a great deal to do with the effectiveness of the technique. I feel that their work on small rice bowls and tea bowls was the most appropriate. These articles were about 4-5 inches in diameter and perhaps 3-4 inches high.

Courtesy of the Museum of Fine Arts, Boston.
Bequest of Charles B. Hoyt (Acq. 50.2014).

Figure 24.4　Chinese Sung dynasty Chi-chou bowl with leaf pattern.

There was one more type of decoration used in Yung Ho, and its method of formation has not been satisfactorily explained as far as I know. This is the leaf temmoku, which is usually a small rice bowl with a deep brown glaze and a perfect pattern of a leaf imposed on the inner surface. Obviously these were not hand painted to represent a leaf, because they are too perfect. You can recognize the species of leaf and see details down to the individual veins. Altogether, several explanations have been given on how to do this, and while I have tried them all, none have worked for me. I have had some luck with the following procedure though. I have taken a damp, pliable natural leaf (a remoistened autumn leaf) and have used this like a floppy rubber stamp. It only needs: first, to be dipped in a slurry of straw ash or iron oxide or titania; and then, to be pressed on the unfired, brown glazed ware. Only the portions of the leaf that stick out from its surface imprint on the base glaze, hence it is necessary to use the bottom surface of the leaf. Nevertheless, while this may sound simple, it is difficult because the leaf has to be of the right degree of flexibility and has to have an appropriate absorption. And, as with all

Chinese wares, the percentage of successful pieces may not have been too high. Another possibility is that it may require a very delicate touch and about ten years of practice.

As a variation on this, a plain leaf can be pressed on a damp glaze or body in order to make an indented pattern, and then the indentations on the dried piece can be filled with a contrasting color. This does not look exactly like the Chinese work, but it can be an attractive decoration.

PHYSICAL DECORATIONS

The use of carving or other impressions of designs on a surface of a pot (in a leather-hard or softer state), can also allow ash glazes to assume a decorative effect. This will make use of the fluidity of ash glazes and it will be found that they readily stop at ridges on pot surfaces, or run along grooves on a surface and in the process fill in indentations. This technique was used by the Chinese in the very early stages of their stoneware and feldspathic glaze development. At that time, rings were made around the necks of large round bottles, and ash glazes were applied above these. In this way all running ceased when the glaze flowed to the ring. An example of this can be seen in the following figure.

Courtesy of the Freer Gallery of Art, Smithsonian Institution, Washington, D.C. 20560 (Acq. 09.331).

Figure 24.5 Chinese Han dynasty tripod vessel.

MAKING USE OF FLUIDITY

It is also possible to use ashes to cause runs on other types of glazes, although this would not be a unique use of ash. Because of the high lime content of wood ash, it could be used above or underneath a glaze to cause enhanced fluidity. I have had this happen more or less by accident while I was testing glazes, but the same effect can be obtained by merely painting pure calcium carbonate over a glaze. Thus I don't think that this would be either a spectacular or worthwhile use of wood ash.

25 THE CONTAMINATION OF ASH

While I don't believe in washing ash itself, I have been converted into being a believer of washing material before it is ashed. This is another important fact which was brought out by Brother Daniel in his book. He correctly emphasizes that we must always be aware of the contamination potential in all of our ashes no matter what variety they are. This contamination may be very obvious, as when one is picking up ashes from a burned house or barn and sees that there are nails and other materials scattered in the ash. Then it is obvious that some of this metal has flaked off into the ash and contaminated it.

However, there are more subtle forms of contamination. If log wood is to be used as an ash material, you would be well advised to go out in the field to observe a logging operation. There you would see: trees being cut down; trees being trimmed of their branches; and tree trunks being dragged or rolled around on the ground. At any rate, there is a high degree of contact between the trunk and the soil, and the bark tends to pick up a good deal of dirt as it is being dragged around. This may or may not be very noticeable on the trunk, depending on its roughness. Similarly the moisture content of the ground and how much manipulation has occurred will affect the contamination. But, no matter how slight it may be, this contamination is a very real problem for us if we are working with firewood, because the ash content of tree wood is rather low—below 1% in many cases. Therefore, if the bark has contributed only one percent of dirt to the weight of the wood, this would be equivalent in quantity to the amount of ash that we would collect; contamination would equal 100% of the ash. This may be the reason that many glaze formulas for ash glazes are extremely confusing. If you consider the composition of an ordinary soil sample to be about the same as the average composition of the earth's crust, then we would have contamination numbers like these:

	EARTH'S CRUST	NY SHALE	OAK ASH	1:1 ASH:SHALE
Silica	60%	65%	2%	33%
Alumina	15%	15%	—	7%
Potash	3%	3%	10%	6%
Soda	3%	1%	4%	2%
Lime	5%	1%	72%	36%
Magnesia	4%	2%	4%	3%
Iron Oxide	6%	7%	—	3%
Titania	1%	1%	—	1%
Phosphate	0.3%	—	6%	3%

From these figures it can be seen that the ash has changed from a basic material (i.e. one loaded with lime) to a glaze-like material, when it is mixed 1:1 with earthy matter.

It is entirely reasonable to assume that the residual ash from the burning of an earth contaminated log might be very close to a usable glaze composition. However, it would be impractical to count on this behavior, because we could never be sure what the earthy contamination was. Therefore, to keep things under control, it would be advisable to use wood that has either been cleaned or has not been in contact with earth. Among the materials that might be desirable from this standpoint are sawdust and chips from a sawmill, a woodshop or any establishment that works with **finished** lumber.

And, as if this case were not bad enough, we must also consider dirt contamination when we are working with ash from hay, straw or vine clippings. The grass or straw may not be dragged over the surface of the earth, but what happens is: during heavy rain storms earth will be splashed up on the stalks of the hay and cereal and will be very tenaciously held there by surface irregularities. If you can remember having dirt present on celery, spinach and lettuce that you buy, then you can imagine this same predicament on hay and wheat. Thus, one must be constantly alert for this situation.

Another area where contamination occurs is at the surface on which a combustible is burned. For example, if someone burns wood in a cast iron or sheet iron furnace, where the metal is frequently cycled in temperature, it will be found that there is a sizable amount of iron oxide flaked off into the ash. One would hope that this particular contamination would not be very great, because after all, iron stoves do not disintegrate that quickly; but it is something to keep in mind.

Also, sometimes clean organic material is burned on a dirt surface and if the ashes are scraped up with some of the surface then they can be grossly contaminated.

Probably the saddest part of the contamination problem is that it is very difficult to be aware of it, because many of the items which contaminate ash are those items which are present to some extent in ash itself. For example, there is always a certain percentage of iron in an ash and thus when you get an added small dollop of iron from a stove, it is not too obvious. Or, when you are burning wood out of doors, the composition of the earth is different only in degree from the composition of the ashes, because after all the plant has obtained its mineral content from the soil. This is unfortunate, but all very true.

If, to this situation, the fact is added that ashes are variable because of the factors which we mentioned before (such as soil, climate and humidity), then it is obvious that there is practically nothing that we can be **sure** of in ash composition. Only one test would seem to be even slightly worthwhile and that is a test firing of an ash button. If a test button of supposedly pure **wood** ash is found to fuse at 1000°C, then one could be very suspicious of gross contamination. But, any lesser degree of contamination would be hard to recognize.

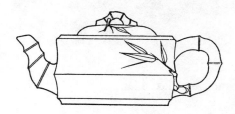

Courtesy of Thomas Clarkson.

Figure 26.1   Contemporary ash glazed jar.

26 X-RAY ANALYSES OF WOOD ASH

Several years ago I did a series of analyses on ashes using the energy dispersive x-ray analysis unit on a scanning electron microscope. This unit allows a rapid analysis of elements with an atomic number higher than sodium in the periodic table, but with rather poor results for sodium itself (due to its low atomic number). The ash samples that I used were obtained by calcining 10 gram samples of materials that I was able to obtain in the local environment. From pieces of lumber and from specimens of trees growing in the neighborhood I took samples of wood, bark, leaves, etc. I also took samples of fern ash and straw ash (and even a sample of cigarette ash). These samples were all fired in a platinum crucible over a Fisher burner until they were well calcined. After that the powdered samples were mounted on a graphite substrate so that there would be a minimum of background. Then they were placed in the scanning electron microscope for analysis. (See THOSE CELADON BLUES, pages 155-157 for a description of the apparatus.)

Because these experiments were done several years ago, the sensitivity was not as good as it might be today. For example, the iron analysis was limited by the fact that the measurement was being taken in a stainless steel chamber and therefore there was some background iron in the readings.

The result of each of the analyses was a graph indicating the relative abundance of the elements in the sample. It is possible to make a rough estimate of the percentages, but it certainly is not at all "accurate." In the following series of examples, three things will be shown for some of the ash samples. First of all, the original chart of the peak heights of the x-ray analyses from the samples will be illustrated. Second, an **estimate** of the percentages that these peaks represent will be made. And third, a comparison with wet chemical analyses on similar samples, as reported by Wolff, will be given. Wolff's analytical report will, of course, be much more accurate than my estimates. There will be a fair degree of disagreement between my results and Wolff's results, and his should be preferred in every case.

Specimen I is spruce ash and the x-ray results are shown in figure 1. The sample that this ash was taken from was a piece of spruce lumber (a 2X4) that had no bark or knot associated with it.

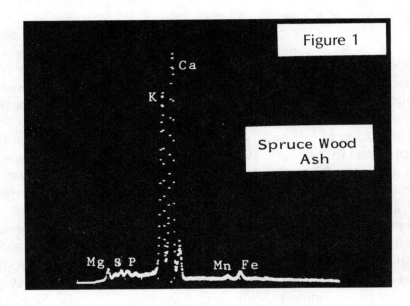

Estimates of the quantities represented by this graph are:

Mg	P	S	K	Ca	Mn	Fe
3	2	2	40	40	5	5

Wolff's analysis from the trunk of a spruce tree is:

11	2.5	2.5	20	34	24	1

The main divergence between Wolff's work and the x-ray estimate is that the potassium:calcium ratio is distorted and there is a large amount of manganese reported in Wolff's sample.

Specimen II is pine ash and the x-ray result is shown in figure 2. A sample of wood from a local pine tree was ashed and used.

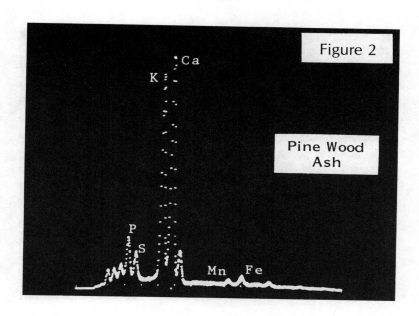

Estimates of the quantities represented by this graph are:

Mg	P	S	K	Ca	Mn	Fe
3	10	7	40	40	2	3

Wolff's results for a pine ash were:

11	6	4	14	54	3	0.1

Here the resemblance between the samples is fairly good, except for the fact that my sample seems to be higher in potassium and iron than Wolff's.

Specimen III is an oak wood ash analysis and the x-ray analysis is shown in figure 3. The sample was take from an oak wood sample from a local tree.

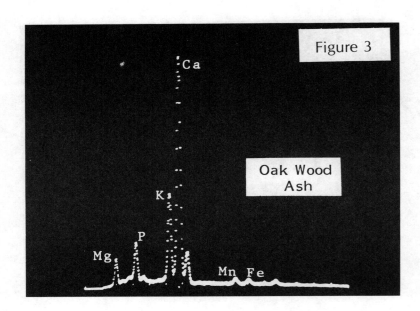

Estimates from this plot are:

Mg	P	S	K	Ca	Mn	Fe
8	10	—	20	40	3	3

For Wolff's analysis of oak trunk wood:

17	17	3	35	22	3	0.6

The main differences in the analyses appear to be that in my sample there is slightly less phosphorus, magnesium and potassium and slightly more calcium and iron.

Specimen IV is a beech wood ash sample using wood taken from a local tree. The x-ray analysis is shown in figure 4.

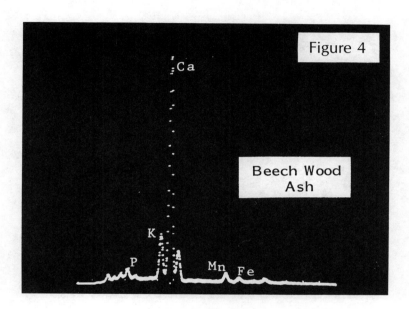

Estimates of this analysis are:

Mg	P	S	K	Ca	Mn	Fe
2	3	1	10	50	4	2

Wolff gives a wet chemical analysis for Beech wood ash as:

12	15	3	31	29	5	1

Wolff's analysis differs from the x-ray analysis in showing a much higher phosphorus level, higher potash and lower calcium.

Just for a relief, let us take a look at two more samples, one of them straw ash and another fern ash. The graph in figure 5 shows the x-ray analysis for oat straw ash.

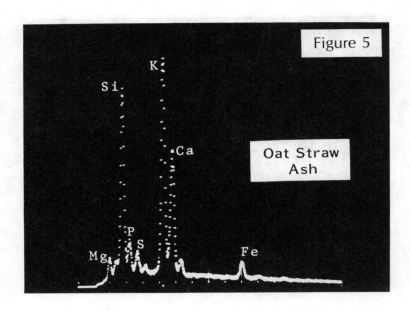

Estimates of the numbers from that plot are:

Mg	Si	P	S	K	Ca	Fe	Cl
4	30	5	5	30	20	5	3

The composition from Wolff's analysis was:

4	47	5	3	26	7	1	4

This is about as good an agreement as we have had in comparisons of Wolff's data and ours.

The last material to be dealt with here is fern ash, and undoubtedly there is a great deal of difference between different varieties of ferns. I used an annual fern and found the results illustrated in figure 6.

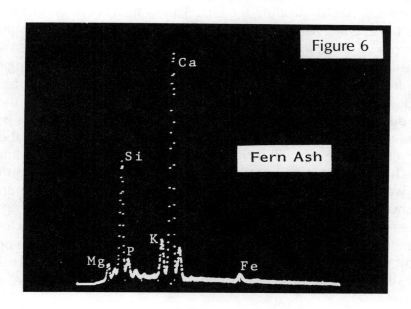

Estimates of this composition are:

Mg	Si	P	S	K	Ca	Fe	Cl
3	30	5	2	10	40	3	1

Whereas Wolff in an analysis gives:

| 6 | 20 | 8 | 3 | 38 | 11 | 1.7 | 8 |

Here the major divergence between the two results is a reversal of the potash to calcium ratio.

The particular numbers from Wolff represent averages from several analyses of the species represented. For example his fern analyses represent the average of 9 samples and the straw analysis is the average from 30 separate analyses. The wood ashes are all averages of results from 6-12 samples.

As an indication of how much deviation there can be in several samples, Wolff has given some ranges for ash compositions. I will just give one sample to illustrate the fact. This is for beech wood ash, and shows the average result for 9 different samples: for potash the numbers went from 25-35%; for soda, from 0.5-3.5%; for lime, from 26-34%; for magnesia from 11-13%; for iron oxide from 0.6-1.9%; for manganese oxide from 0-9%; for phosphorus pentoxide from 11-17%; for sulfur dioxide from 2-4%; and for silica, from 1.4-3.9%. Undoubtedly there is some difference in the quality of the analytical results, but that is probably not the most important variable in these numbers. The actual oxide content of the tree ash will have deviated this much because of differing soils, climates, moisture conditions and exposures to the sun. So once again we see that the ash content of a material is not a definite number. This should not be a big surprise to us though, because we certainly realize that there is a real difference in other products too. If we look at commercial feldspars, for example, a potash feldspar may have a potash content varying from 8-13%; an alumina content varying from 16-20%; and a silica content varying from 65-72%.

It is hoped that this collection of numbers will help you appreciate the range of compositions to be found in wood ashes.

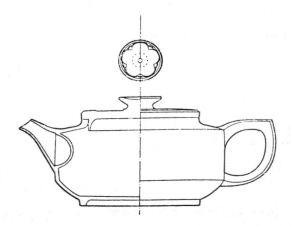

27   INDIVIDUAL ASH INGREDIENTS

There are at least two ways to examine the separate influences of the several ash components. One of these is to test each component by itself, and the other is to vary the concentration of each component in a standard glaze. Both of these techniques will be used here to help in understanding the nature of ashes and ash glazes.

TESTING INDIVIDUAL COMPONENTS

It is possible to learn a great deal about the individual elements in ash glazes simply by using each of them by itself on a body to see how it reacts during the normal firing process. While the interactions **between** these compounds are missed in such tests, still you can get some idea of how the individual elements do their job. That is what has been investigated in this section. Each of the elements present in an ash has been enumerated and then each one has been applied to the surface of a ceramic body and then has been fired and observed.

From these observations it is hoped that you will get a rough idea of what elements should be used in a synthetic ash glaze and what elements may be ignored. In this way, when a synthetic ash glaze is made up it will be no more complicated than is necessary. However, with some elements, it is difficult to view them individually, since they are always accompanied by some other element. For example, sodium cannot be applied to a body surface as just sodium; it has to be applied as sodium chloride, sodium carbonate or sodium sulfate. Thus with sodium chloride two results are observed, one due to sodium and the other due to chloride. But, by doing a series of sodium salts and a series of chloride salts, it is possible to deduce what influence the sodium ion has and what influence the chloride ion has.

There are other techniques, but I don't know whether it is necessary to go to any extremes. For example, sodium hydroxide could be used in an effort to isolate the effect due to sodium; or, we could use ammonium chloride for the same purpose with chloride; but I don't believe that these tests would be foolproof either.

ELEMENTS TO CONSIDER

Obviously, each ash will have its own particular combination of elements, and sometimes the concentrations will vary widely, as with the high concentration of silica in straw ash when compared to wood ash, but, all of the important elements in ash will be discussed here.

A key question is: what are the **unimportant** elements in ashes? My answer is: elements which do not have a detectable effect in an ash glaze. Good examples of this are aluminum and titanium. Although aluminum may be occasionally present to the extent of a percent or so in ash, this is not going to have a significant effect in a glaze which is in contact with a clay body containing about 20% alumina. The reaction of glaze and body will be sufficient to wash out the effect of any small quantity of aluminum in ash. The same goes for titanium. With 0.1-1% titanium in body clay, any small amount of this element in ash can be neglected.

Therefore, the elements to be concerned about in ash glazes are:

> Potassium
> Sodium
> Calcium
> Magnesium
> Iron
> Manganese
> Phosphorus
> Sulfur
> Silicon
> Chlorine
> (Carbonate)

Here are descriptions of the individual tests that I have run. Examples of some of these tests can be seen in the illustrations.

1. Sodium chloride washed on an iron containing body produces a medium brown varnish-like glaze. The same is true for potassium chloride.

2. Sodium phosphate washed on a body results in a tan, varnish-like glaze.

3. When calcium carbonate is brushed on a body, a drippy, clear glaze results if the layer is thin.

4. But, when calcium **chloride** is washed on a body, a light tan varnish-like glaze results.

5. Iron chloride washed on a body gives a dull, dark brown finish. While with manganese chloride a medium-brown, varnish-like glaze results.

6. When sodium sulfate is washed on a body, a brown, matte surface results.

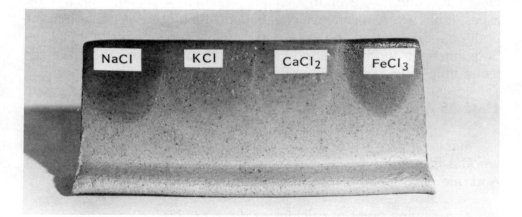

Figure 27.1 A stoneware plaque with examples of salt washes.

And so forth. There are dozens of possibilities, but not too many have significance for our study of ash glazes. It is extremely easy to try these tests, so if you are curious, make an attempt. Just be sure that you thoroughly **dry** all of your pieces before you fire them.

Naturally some of these tests don't do us much good at all, and a case in point has to do with phosphate. The phosphate content of ashes usually varies from 1-10%, however its importance is not in its use as an individual substance, but as a component of a mixture. So, when sodium phosphate is placed on a body, although an interesting effect is produced, it has no relation to the real world of ashes where only a small percentage of phosphate is present in a mixture. Similarly, if calcium phosphate is applied by itself on the surface of a pot, it doesn't melt at all, whereas a small percentage of calcium phosphate in a glaze can have a remarkable effect on the final product.

There has been some fallout from these tests though, and I think that the two most useful results have been those dealing with the calcium ion and with the chloride ion. Since calcium is present in wood ash in such a high percentage, it is useful to see what happens when it is applied by itself. And in this case we see that calcium (from the carbonate or oxide) is tied up with the high surface tension effect (the beading up of the glaze). Therefore we can feel comfortable with the observation that this is one of calcium's roles in ash.

An interesting result is also tied up with the action of chloride ion. Here it is found that, even though it is present in small amounts in most ashes, it has a very distinctive effect. It apparently causes the iron in the body to move around and to give the familiar brown edge at the glaze-body interface and in bare body areas. From these observations we can feel a little more certain about the action of chloride ion in ashes.

LIME AS A REFRACTORY MATERIAL

Since calcium oxide often represents half of the oxide content of wood ash, it is important that we understand all of its characteristics. And one of its main features is a high fusion temperature.

The melting point of calcium oxide is **2572°C**.

Thus there can be no mistaking the fact that this is a refractory material. However, we also run into the seemingly contrary information that calcium oxide (or calcium carbonate) is a flux. But it is a **flux** only when it is used in combination with other materials, such as feldspar, kaolin or silica. Alone, it is a refractory substance. So we have to face the fact that as we use higher and higher percentages of calcium oxide in our glaze mixtures, we get more and more refractory glazes.

As we have seen in the chapter on the composition of wood ashes, there is a high lime content in most wood ashes. The calcium oxide content of wood ash usually runs from 30-60%. This puts wood ash in the range of composition of pure calcium carbonate (which has a calcium oxide content of 56%).

My words of warning are with regard to the practice of putting very high percentages of wood ash in glaze mixtures. If we use the approximation from the above paragraph, then we can see that a glaze containing 50% wood ash could be equivalent to a glaze with about 30% calcium carbonate (which is a fairly high percentage). It is a rare glaze which will have that much of a single flux.

This leads to the confusing situation where a high wood ash glaze actually has a dry appearance; not because it has too little flux, but because it has too much. When such a glaze is inspected, the first thing that comes to mind is that there is not enough flux in it because the glaze is too dry, while actually the reverse is true. Because the flux is calcium oxide, it has led to refractoriness in the glaze.

I believe that the safest course to follow in making an ash glaze is to consider ash to be calcium carbonate and use it in the same percentages that you would calcium carbonate. Then if you run into trouble you can be fairly sure what the problem is and what the solution is. If you are using 20% ash in a glaze and the glaze does not fuse, you can assume that the trouble is due to too little flux and you can add additional wood ash in the next trial. On the other hand, if you add 50% wood ash to a glaze and it doesn't melt you must consider the possibility that you have added too much wood ash.

THE EFFECT OF INDIVIDUAL ASH INGREDIENTS IN GLAZE BLENDS

Now let's consider how ash components affect complete glazes. Instead of using individual compounds, let us make glazes and then vary the elements in these glazes. However, before starting, let's take a look at the common elements found in ashes and describe what their effects are. Then we can decide whether they are unique to ashes and whether we want to resort only to ash when we want these effects.

1. Silicon - The amount of silica in wood ash is rather low and usually only amounts to a few percent. In straw ash however, we may encounter up to 50% silica. But the question is: is this a unique material, or can we fabricate a glaze with the same properties just by using the **mineral** silica? Probably the most unique characteristic of silica from ash would be its small particle size. The silica is presumably well dispersed in ash, and unless the ash has been fired to a high temperature, so that fritting occurs, then the silica would be present in a powdery state. If its physical state is its most important aspect, it would be possible to add a pulverized mineral raw material (such as Minulsil-5) to the glaze batch. Presumably you would then get the same effect that you would from the finely divided silica in ash.

2. Calcium in ash is usually found as calcium carbonate because of the reaction of calcium oxide with carbon dioxide from the air or from the combustion process. If we have to use calcium carbonate in a glaze, there should be no expectation at all that **mineral** derived calcium carbonate couldn't work just as well as the "natural" calcium carbonate that would be found in wood ash. The same would hold true for magnesium carbonate. The only reason that either of these alkaline earth elements might be different in wood ash is that they might be in the form of calcium phosphate or sulfate also (or the magnesium salts). However these, too, could be provided by mineral sources.

3. Alkalies in ashes, and especially the potassium salts, are very interesting to us. Here we find a particularly unique component of wood ash. Normally we add alkalies to glazes as feldspars or as frits that are relatively insoluble. So the potassium that we add to a glaze as a potash feldspar is completely different from the majority of the potassium or sodium that would be added to a glaze through wood ash. In ash the alkalies normally are present in the form of carbonates (plus sulfates, phosphates and chlorides). Naturally this is not unique. If we wish to duplicate an ash result without using wood ash, we can get the soluble

alkali effect by adding potassium carbonate, sodium chloride, or some other salt of theirs to a glaze batch. At this point I will not state whether or not this is desirable, I will just comment that it is possible to perform this same function by using mineral sources instead of wood ash.

4. Colorants are another category of materials found in wood ash. Although there are probably small amounts of titania, vanadium, copper and chromium in wood ash, they are not present in significant amounts. The two coloring elements that we do need to consider are iron and manganese. Although iron oxide is usually reported in wood ash and manganese is seldom reported, we find on examining the detailed information from Wolff that manganese can actually be present in higher concentrations than iron. But this is not too complicated for our substitution considerations because the iron and manganese may easily be added to a glaze batch as the oxides. Fortunately the nature of the oxides added will not be too important, for our firing technique will decide what the ultimate oxidation state of these two elements is. We may put in ferric oxide and manganese dioxide, but if they are fired in reduction, they both will end up as divalent materials. Again, the important criteria is the fineness of the particles.

5. Of the anions present in ashes, phosphate is the most intriguing because of its effect on coloration through phase separation. But there is no uniqueness to the phosphate in ash and it may be added to a glaze either as the mineral apatite or as bone ash.

6. Sulfur in the form of sulfate is present in ashes. There it has a negative reputation as an ash ingredient because some sulfates tend to decompose at high temperatures with the release of sulfur dioxide or trioxide, and these cause bubbling. Also, in reduction it can cause trouble as the source of sulfide in glazes. So the presence of sulfates in ashes may only be of negative importance to us. Because of sulfate's disagreeable characteristics I doubt if we would voluntarily want to add much sulfate to a glaze.

Summarizing, of all the elements which are found in ashes, it is apparent that the so-called "natural" elements are not unique in any way. They may definitely be replaced by adding appropriate minerals to a glaze. The only possible unique aspect of ash components is their fine particle size and their ready reactivity because of this characteristic. Other than that, as we will indicate in the chapter on the fabrication of synthetic ashes, it is entirely possible to make an acceptable synthetic ash using minerals.

To avoid confusion, let me assert that some elements may be either major **or** minor constituents of ashes. For example, there is the case of silica. Though it may be a minor constituent of wood ash, it is a major component of straw ash and therefore we will not consider it in this chapter on minor constituents.

We will discuss here the elements which are usually minor in all types of ash. These will include the following. Chloride, sulfate, phosphate, manganese, iron, titanium, aluminum and sodium. Obviously many more elements are **present**, however, because they are in low quantities they will have no noticeable influence. Thus we are only examining elements which are found in large enough quantities to have an effect and yet cannot be considered to be major constituents of ashes.

To start off, let us eliminate some of those items which have already been mentioned. First of all, consider alumina. The concentration of alumina in ash is probably always small (below 5%). And, since alumina is always a rather major constituent of glazes, it will be added from other parts of the glaze and thus the presence or absence of alumina in ash in amounts up to 5% can be ignored because its importance will be washed out by other additions of alumina.

The same is probably true for sodium. Sodium will always be present in ash in quantities of 1-5%, but its effect is going to be smothered by the presence of high percentages of potassium. It is true that in certain plants grown near the sea or in high soda deserts the sodium in ash may be quite high, but in our normal operations we will not be dealing with such plants and their ashes. So let's eliminate sodium from our list of minor elements.

One true **minor** element which is always present to a small extent in ash, and which has quite a significant effect in glazes, is the chloride ion. Its quantity in wood ash is probably only about 0.1-1%, yet chloride has a remarkable influence on glazes because of the fact that some chlorides are very volatile. Thus we find that the chloride has a real effect on the migration of iron in both the body and in the glaze. And if we make up a series of glazes with and without chloride content, the first thing we will note is that chloride affects the movement of iron, especially in the body, and the classical result is that a brown varnish appears below the glaze level on the bare body. This is a key to showing the presence of chloride in a wood ash or any other constituent of a glaze.

Sulfate is another minor element, although I am not quite sure how significant it is. One tends to think of sulfate as an undesirable material in a glaze, but I do not know of any particularly bad influence that it may have on ash glazes. Additional experiments with sulfate, using particular examples, could evaluate this effect.

Phosphate is a material which is always present in ashes. But, in this case, in certain wood ashes, the phosphate may reach quite high levels. Instead of being in the neighborhood of 1% it may end up as high as 10% or more. With sizable percentages of ash in a glaze this is a remarkable amount and can cause startling effects. The most commonly observed result of phosphate additions is that of opalization. Phosphate is a glass former like silica, but in mixtures with silica, an immiscibility is found (just as is found with oil and water). The two glasses do not always blend together but often separate; and this may only happen at low temperatures. They mix well at high temperatures and then segregate during a cooling operation or a reheating (striking) action. This gives an opal appearance where one glass appears as tiny droplets suspended in the other medium. This is much the same thing that happens in mayonnaise, where tiny oil droplets are dispersed in vinegar. This feature, though, will be very dependent on the concentration of the phosphate and the composition of the glass and is not always predictable. It **is** something to watch out for.

COLORING AGENTS IN ASH GLAZES

Of course iron is a colorant in ashes although it is not present in as high a quantity as one might suspect. It is seldom present at much over 1% of the ash and therefore the iron from the ash is no more worrisome than the iron in clays that one adds to glazes, since clays frequently have 1-2% iron content.

Titania as a minor component is probably most important for its influence on the iron. Unfortunately, it is difficult to analyze for titania and it is commonly ignored in ash analyses. This is not to say that it is not present, but it is infrequently evaluated. Thus we are left a little bit in the dark when it comes to titania. The only evidence that I have concerning titania is from x-ray data. Using this technique I found that titania is always at a lower concentration than iron in common ashes.

Manganese is a real "sleeper." Again, it is not ordinarily measured in ash, but when it is, it is startling to learn that 1-5% may be present. If manganese is present in the form of the divalent ion it evidently is not much of a colorant, but as it becomes oxidized, it becomes more noticeable. And frequently in our ash glazes we see a brownish coloration which is slightly different from the brownish appearance that we get from iron. The iron brown has a yellowish tint, while the manganese brown is somewhat reddish. One should definitely be on the lookout for the effects of manganese, especially in **wood** ash.

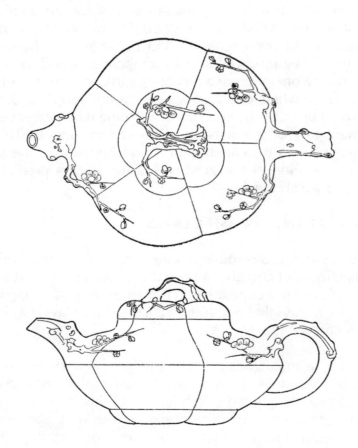

28 DIFFUSION IN ASH GLAZES

Anyone who has made an ash glaze on an iron-containing body will have noticed the extension of the coloration below the glaze level on the outside of the ceramic piece (as can be seen in the figure). Whenever a glaze is made of **unwashed** wood ash and other materials, the glaze will have some of the alkali in solution in the glaze slip. This portion of the alkali will move into the body, and in the liquid state will diffuse below the glaze level. The alkali containing solution will "wick" into the porous body and will provide us with a sort of "salt glaze" effect in an area just below the normal glaze.

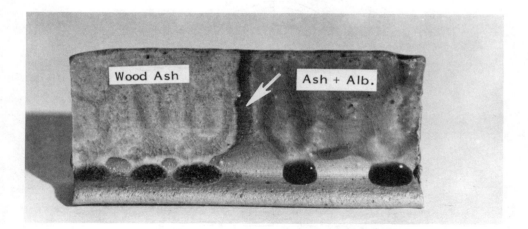

Figure 28.1   An ash glazed plaque showing the brown varnish effect (arrow) due to alkali absorption by the body.

This "liquid state" diffusion occurs where the liquid is water. In this instance diffusion occurs merely because of the porosity of the body and the capillarity effect. But, there is also another type of diffusion which will take place during the firing.

The firing diffusion is a so-called "solid state" reaction. The alkali at high temperatures will be dry and will possibly have reacted with the body. After this there will be a slow diffusion (increasing with increasing temperatures) of the alkali in the body in all directions. Alkali will diffuse outward into the glaze, it will diffuse inward towards the center of the body, it will diffuse downward and upward. However, in only one case will this diffusion be noticeable, and that is in the downward direction—if we have an unglazed foot on our piece. Here we will see an extension of the salt-glaze type effect far below the glaze level on the body.

In addition to the simple diffusion of alkalies there will also be the movement of some of the iron of the body (depending on how much is present). Thus if you have a body with about one percent iron oxide in it, you will see a brown, glossy rim down below the glaze area. This is caused by the presence in the wood ash of not only alkali, but soluble halides, sulfates and phosphates. Iron chloride is fairly volatile and will move towards the surface where it will leave a brown ring around the base.

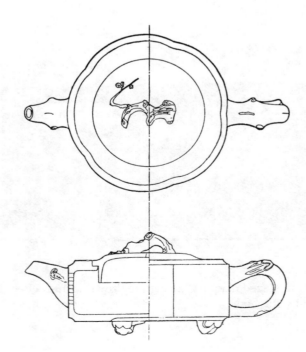

29 OXIDATION AND REDUCTION

The story of oxidation and reduction in ash glazes is principally the story of celadons. Although this subject has been covered quite thoroughly in the book, **THOSE CELADON BLUES**, it should be considered here too, with a brief discussion.

Since ashes are derivatives of the soil on which a plant has grown, they will naturally be similar to other natural inorganic raw materials. However, there will be some slight differences in proportions of the minor elements in ash glazes. Of the colorants, in concentrations sufficient to alter the glaze, we probably only need to consider two, and these are iron and manganese.

It is true that every element on earth can be found in ash, just as they can in earthy minerals, but the concentrations of elements such as copper, titanium, chromium and vanadium are low enough not to affect the color of a glaze, especially when they are masked by strong colors from iron and manganese.

REDUCTION AND IRON

The iron in ash (which is due to the ash components and not contamination) should be uniformly distributed throughout the ash. However the contamination from materials such as nails or barbed wire or chunks of earth bring us to the problem of speck and spot formation in ash glazes. This is currently a real problem because of the ubiquitous occurrence of iron in our civilization. This is truly an iron age today, and as far as our glazes are concerned we have to be on the lookout to avoid

166

speckly results—unless you are looking for a rough appearing glaze. However, if you do want to be sure of a smooth, uniform celadon from an ash glaze, then by all means resort to sieving and a thorough ball milling to pulverize particles that may be high in iron content. You might even try running a strong magnet over the coarse ash to pick out odd bits of iron metal.

Titania will be a problem only from the contamination aspect because it commonly occurs in ash at concentrations of less than 1%, while it is present to the extent of 1-2% in all earths. The biggest dilemma with respect to titanium is that it is rarely reported in ash analyses. It used to be rather difficult to analyze for titania, and it is probably always rather low in concentration in ashes; so it was commonly neglected in otherwise thorough analyses. It is unfortunate that this is true, because as glazers we are all too aware of its habit of changing blue celadons to greens. As a practical matter, a celadon glaze test might be the simplest and most accurate way to gauge the presence of titanium. If you get a good blue celadon in a high ash glaze, then there can't be much titania present.

BLUES

Two characteristics of wood ash help us in the formation of blue celadons. In the first place, as mentioned, there is never very much titanium in wood ash, which is a plus in favor of celadon blue formation. Also, one generally finds 5-10% phosphate in wood ash and this is a desirable material for blue celadon formation. If we use anywhere from 10-50% wood ash in a glaze, then the percentage of phosphate that will be in the glaze will be sizable and will have a positive influence on the production of both blues and opals.

MANGANESE

Manganese is a bit of a sleeper in ashes and in ash glazes. Wolff quotes figures going from 0.3% manganese oxide in deciduous tree ash to 28.5% in fir tree trunk ash. As an indication that this is not accidental, another report lists 24% manganese oxide in spruce tree trunk ash. Obviously there are highly variable and often high manganese concentrations in ashes from tree trunks. My own analyses, via energy dispersive x-ray analyses, also recognizes sizable manganese percentages in tree ash analyses, but not quite as high as those reported in Wolff's work.

During my analyses of ash from 9 different woods (including pine, cedar, spruce, redwood and several deciduous trees), manganese appeared most of the time and in amounts approximately equal to the quantities of iron in the ash. An estimate of the **maximum** manganese content would be around 5-10%, judging from the peak heights. An example of the presence of manganese in a wood ash can be seen in the following reproduction of an x-ray graph of common wood ash.

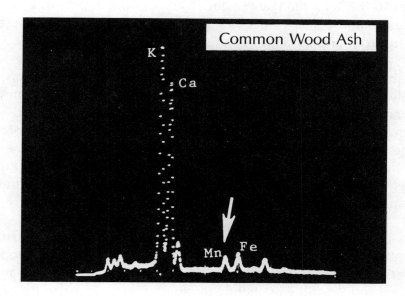

Even though manganese is not usually considered a strong coloring agent in the divalent form, at these high concentrations it certainly can be, and would lead to brown colorations when it is present in high percentages (accompanied by iron). I believe that the iron-manganese couple results in deeper colors than a simple additive effect would lead one to expect.

Theoretically, in the oxidized state (at plus three) manganese should give rise to some brilliant colors such as blues and purples. But, at the high temperatures at which our glazes will be fired, it is possible that manganese will thermally decompose from the plus three to the plus two state, and will therefore give browns rather than blues or purples. The conditions favorable to the brilliant colors, namely the presence of large ions (such as lead and barium) in high concentrations, means that these colors are unlikely, since we will not have large percentages of such elements in our high fired ash glazes.

In a page of analytical results from wood ash analyses, in almost every case Wolff lists higher oxide concentrations (by a factor of 5 or 10) for manganese compared to iron. For example, for oak wood ash, he gives a percentage of 2.7 for manganese and 0.6 for iron; in birch wood ash he lists 8.7% for manganese and 0.9% for iron; in pine ash, 3.3% for manganese and 0.1% for iron; in spruce ash, 24% for manganese and 1.4% for iron; and so on.

If these proportions hold true in all wood analyses then it is quite unlikely that we will get celadons which are due to the iron from wood ash, because the manganese would certainly mask that color. When celadons do show up from the wash of a body with a thin coat of ash, it may be that the celadon color results from iron originating in the body rather than the iron in the ash. And, the fact that thick glazes of pure ash brushed on a body often turn out to be a deep brown, may illustrate the manganese content of the ash rather than the iron content.

As a matter of fact, the manganese influence may account for an observation that I have made on a natural wood ash/synthetic wood ash comparison. My synthetic wood ash (which came very close to average analytical results) still was slightly different when it came to the appearance of thick sections of both glazes. Looking closely at the two samples, I can now see that the difference could be due to a relatively high manganese content in the natural ash. In my synthetic glaze there is no brown coloration in the thicker dribbles, but only a deeper green celadon. But, in the natural ash glaze, where there are dribbles (particularly on the inside) there is a definite brownish cast and some devitrification and this may represent the presence of 5-10% manganese oxide in the natural ash.

30 PHASE SEPARATION

In ash glazes, the effect of phase separation, devitrification or crystallization (whichever terminology you prefer) is very likely to occur, because the characteristics of ashes that favor phase separation are many. For example, there are some specific materials which tend to cause opal-type phase separation in glass (such as the chlorides, sulfates and phosphates), and we find these present in almost every type of ash. In addition, wood ash usually has a very high content of lime, and since ash is commonly used in large percentages in glaze mixtures, this high lime content will lead to very fluid glasses which are prone to devitrify on slow cooling.

One of the most fascinating observations that can be made on ash glazes is the tendency for them to form clear glasses when they are present as thin coatings on a ceramic and the tendency for them to crystallize when they are in thick layers. Obviously, where the glaze is thin, calcium has reacted strongly with silica and alumina from the body to form a glaze which is high in those two elements and hence is viscous and glassy. But, in thicker layers, calcium is further removed from the body and so the glaze composition in these regions is higher in lime and thus is closer to a compound such as calcium silicate (wollastonite) or calcium alumino-silicate (anorthite) which can then crystallize. And indeed these crystals are frequently found in high lime glazes as can be seen in following figure.

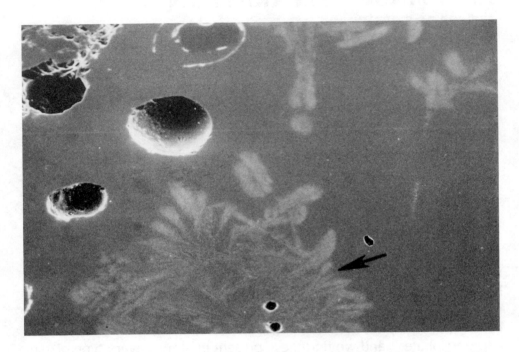

Figure 30.1 Anorthite crystals (arrow) seen in a cross sectional view of a Chien temmoku glaze.

If wood ash is mixed with materials which contain much more silica than alumina, this same type of crystallization will result, although it will not be so dependent on the thickness of the glaze. Such a high silica, high lime glaze will also provide an environment which allows the phosphate to be effective as an opalizing agent. Such a glaze with a few percent phosphate in it will readily become opalescent, with a true separation of two different glass phases. One of the phases will be high in silica and the other will be high in phosphate, the two being immiscible when fluid.

Aluminum is a critical element when one is trying to **prevent** phase separation or devitrification in glasses and glazes. Therefore, if you do not want either of these effects, it is appropriate to add kaolin to the ash glaze batch. Nevertheless it is also true that the addition of alumina will tend to transmute the glaze from a traditional "ashy" type, into a rather ordinary type. Hence one must use discretion in making these additions and add no more than is necessary to prevent gross devitrification (if it happens that you do not like this effect). Since I do like the runniness and the attack of ash on the body, I would tend to put as little alumina or kaolin as possible in an ash glaze and thus avoid destroying this "ashiness," which to me is the basic aim in making these glazes.

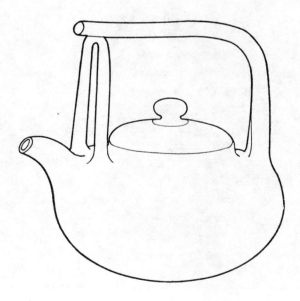

Courtesy of Thomas Clarkson

Figure 31.1 Contemporary ash glazed covered jar.

31 THE BLEACHED BODY LAYER

If an ash wash is placed over an iron-containing body in a very thin layer, it can be seen that the body, in certain regions underneath the wash, is brownish colored. In other regions though, there is a whitening effect, depending on the thickness of the wash layer. This whitening can be observed even when the ash is mixed with clay or feldspar. It is apparent that the brown layer is connected with the soluble materials in the ash, but the origin of the bleached layer is a little more puzzling.

Figure 31.2 Ash glazed plaque showing bleached areas (arrows) underneath the glaze.

It is to be expected that a series of experiments would show us what the cause of the bleach layer is even though they may not tell us what the mechanism is. If we take some of the separate components of an ash and paint each one separately over a body, we can soon observe which elements in an ash are responsible for the bleaching.

The potash, as was noted in the chapter on salt washes, does not cause bleaching, but instead causes a migration of the body iron. And the anions do not appear to do it either, although there is one of them that comes close. This is the phosphate ion. While sodium carbonate, potassium carbonate and sodium chloride cause browning and glossing with an iron-containing ceramic surface, a sodium phosphate wash will not have this effect. It does cause a glossing of the surface, but it does not cause any browning (nor does it actually reduce the color of the body). Still, it gives a pale non-darkened glossy surface. In fact, of all of the solubles that I have tried on 2% iron bodies, none of them tended to cause a whitening effect. Silica, too, does not have a bleaching effect, and I assume that alumina would not because it is too refractory to react. However, there is one other possibility. **Lime** will cause this bleaching effect. If one puts a thin wash of calcium carbonate on a 2% iron body, the effect is much like that observed with an ash wash. There is beading up, there is a lot of crazing, and there is even a slight devitrification in some areas. In addition, at certain optimum thicknesses of this wash and of the resulting glaze, there is a definite whitening of the body, where it becomes lighter colored than it would without a glaze present.

Figure 31.3 Although not too obvious in this photograph, there is body bleaching under both limestone and ash washed areas.

I assume that this is the same effect that Seger has talked about extensively in dealing with the color of bricks. A hundred years ago he observed that the presence of calcium carbonate in a high iron brick would cause the color to bleach. Nevertheless, the explanations that I have seen so far are not very convincing as far as an interpretation of the bleaching is concerned. One might expect that the lime would react with the silica and alumina in the body to form a glass, and because of the observation of the green (celadon) glaze on the surface of the bodies I have washed with calcium carbonate, one assumes that the reaction has also gobbled up some iron. However, whether there is an actual strong movement of iron from the body into the glaze, leaving the body with a deficit of iron, is not too obvious from anything that I have either read or observed.

THE CHUN BLEACHED LAYER

Chinese Chun wares are high fired stoneware ceramics with beautiful blue opal celadon glazes on them. They originated in North China during the Sung dynasty (about 1000 AD), and since a fair amount of phosphate is found in the glaze it is suspected that they were made using ash as one raw material. In addition to the opalescence found in the glaze, another distinctive feature of Chun ware is a white body layer located next to the glaze. This white layer is not a slip layer, but is evidently a reaction zone between the body and the glaze. It is remarkable for being almost pure white and it contrasts strongly with the rather dirty color of the body. As far as I know, this situation has never been explained adequately either, and it is possible that this may be related to our ash case, for some of the Chun glazes are high in lime as well as phosphate.

At the present time I have a strong hunch that the bleached layer is due to an ion exchange reaction between calcium oxide (or calcium carbonate) and the ferrous oxide (or silicate) which colors the body. According to this theory, it is only in the crystalline form that the bleaching occurs. When iron is in a glassy state, it is a relatively pale color that is green in low concentrations and brown in high concentrations. However, when iron is associated with a crystal as it would in iron oxide or iron silicate, then it is a black to grey color and is a deeper hue for the same amount of iron.

My feeling is: when calcium is present in high concentrations, as in a plain ash or a high ash glaze, it can exchange with ferrous iron to give a lightly colored calcium oxide or silicate and a lightly colored iron glass, with much less color than in the previous condition.

Since titanium seems to be intimately tied up with deep iron colors, it is possible that there is a reaction of calcium with titania in a similar way.

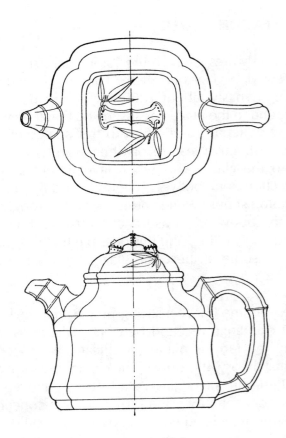

32   THE DURABILITY OF ASH GLAZES

The durability of glazes is important to us for two reasons. In the first instance, there is the possibility for the release of chemicals into food or liquids placed in a container, and this is the paramount reason for worrying about durability. The second durability question of importance to us is the case of the quality of the glaze with regard to its tendency to deteriorate with age in normal household use—such as dishwashing.

Fortunately, the importance of chemical release will not affect the use of ash glazes unless other undesirable components such as lead or barium are used. The natural components of wood ash are unlikely under normal circumstances to provide toxic releases to anyone using a utensil that has been coated with an ash glaze. If other, dangerous materials, such as lead, barium or cadmium are added to the glaze, then it should be considered to be hazardous, just as ordinary glazes would be under the same circumstances. In such a case appropriate measures should be taken to avoid the release of these elements.

The physical deterioration of an ash glaze is another matter however, and this is worth a short investigation on our part.

Whenever a glaze is made which is rather high in alkali, there is a possibility that this glaze may be non-durable. Since wood ash may have a high concentration of potash this makes ash glazes a little worrisome for us. If we make an ash glaze by simply putting an ash wash on a ceramic body, then there is a chance for poor durability if the glaze has a moderate thickness. This is related to the same phenomenon we have noted before. When very thin washes of ash are applied, glazes will be formed which are rather transparent and glassy. On the other hand if we make a rather thick wash of ash on a ceramic body, then there will be a tendency for devitrification and this same bent towards devitrification can lead to poor durability, because the devitrification is due to a high alkali-alkaline earth concentration near the surface of the thick glaze.

When we do put a thin ash wash on the body and if the body is a normal one (with a high concentration of alumina), then the ash materials will react with the alumina and silica of the body to provide a glassy glaze which is fairly durable because of a good alumina content. Anytime we have a **glassy** glaze with a moderate alumina content, we will find that we have good durability. In **glasses**, for instance, we find that the presence of 2-3% alumina in the glass will provide excellent durability. (However, if we go too far, and add too much alumina, so that there is devitrification, then of course we do not have a glassy material, but that is another problem.)

When an ash containing a high percentage of calcium and potassium is put on a body in a thick layer, there will be a good reaction at the glaze-body interface, but further out into the glaze there will be higher and higher concentrations of potassium and calcium. The calcium in particular will lead to crystallite formation and these high calcium compounds found on the surface will not be as durable as the good glass which is in contact with the aluminous body. An example can be seen in the photograph.

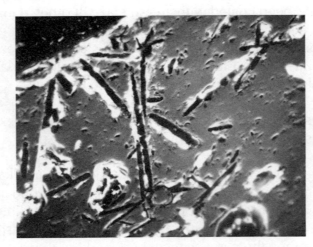

Figure 32.1   Cross section of a glaze showing calcium silicate crystals growing near the surface (300x).

In the case of **glazes** applied to a ceramic body, we are back into a rather standard situation. If wood ash is added to a normal porcelain glaze composition, using the ash as a substitute for whiting, then it will be found that the end product will not be greatly different from an ordinary glaze of the same formulation **with** whiting. Thus there is no gross difference due to the peculiar nature of wood ash, causing it to be differentiated from normal high temperature glazes. And, since glazes fired in the region of 1250°C usually have good durability, we will find that glazes made with ash and fired to this same temperature range will also have acceptable durability, and we will not have to worry about deterioration under normal circumstances.

In conclusion, may I comment that I have never had a problem with ash glazes as far as durability is concerned. The glazes which were of good quality were no more of a problem than other good quality glazes. And, the glazes which were rather unusual (read lumpy), were not applied on articles which would be used for the consumption or storage of food. In the latter case any slight iridescence might even be taken as a desirable quality.

Courtesy Corning Museum of Glass

Figure 33.1 Deep green colored seventeenth century bottle made from sand and wood ash.

33 WOOD ASH AND GLASS

A short time ago at a Corning Glass Museum lecture on "European Glass of the 17th Century," Dwight Lanmon discussed the changes and difficulties that glassmakers ran into when they started manipulating the woodash that was a basic raw material for glasses of that era. The nominal composition of a common glass at that time was sand (of as pure a quality as feasible) plus wood ash. While it was possible to locate sand deposits which were fairly pure, unfortunately an average wood ash contained a percent or two of iron oxide and a sizable amount of manganese. Hence, no matter how pure the sand that was used, if untreated wood ash was also employed, then the glass would have a green or amber tint depending on the ratio of iron to manganese, and depending on the type of firing conditions—whether oxidizing or reducing. This coloration was a big problem for the glassmakers who were trying to copper wheel engrave glass. They wanted to have as thick a glass as possible so that copper wheel engraving could be more exotic (with deeper cuts). But, when a thick glass was used, the color would be too dark because of ash impurities.

Obviously some thinker then went to work and separated ash into its components. The simplest separation would be that due to slurrying ash in water. The extraction of the solubles from the ash led to a solution which contained much of the flux from the ash and practically none of the coloring materials. It was noted by those glassmakers that the evaporate from the liquid was a potent glass flux, and if just this flux were mixed with silica it could give a glass. (The approximate composition of the solubles from a typical wood ash can be seen in the x-ray scan shown in the next figure.)

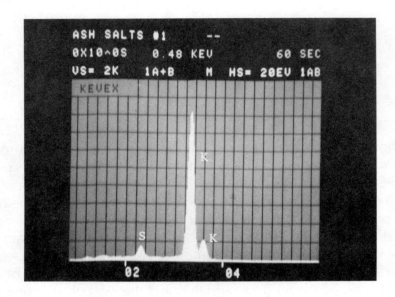

Figure 33.2   EDXR analysis of wood ash solubles.

The main problem though, was that a glass made from sand and wood ash solubles contained principally potash, soda and silica with little lime. This would not give a very durable glass and in fact the glassmakers found that the resulting glass was unacceptable. It would start dissolving on the surface and an effect known as "crizzling" would occur in a short time (reference: Robert Brill). Crizzling involved a reaction of atmospheric moisture with the surface of the alkali silicate glass, and the preferential solution of the alkalies and the deposit of a high silica surface. When such a piece dried, the high silica surface would shrink and cause very fine crazing. In a dry atmosphere the crazed layer would flake off and there would be a rapid destruction of the glass surface in the normal cycle of weather, from winter to summer or from rainy weather to dry weather. Naturally such glass was not acceptable for commercial applications. A specimen of an antique glass suffering from the crizzling phenomenon can be seen in the following photograph.

Courtesy of the Corning Museum of Glass

Figure 33.3 Seventeenth century goblet showing an advanced stage of crizzling.

The composition of one crizzled glass was:

Silica	76.0%
Alumina	0.5%
Lime	0.2%
Potash	18.7%

In two different locations in Europe, two separate solutions were found for the problem. On the Continent, limestone was added to the glass batch and this was found to provide enough durability so that a good glass could be obtained. This is the parent glass for our modern soda-lime glass which is the basis for both bottle and window glass today. Pure sand plus alkali washed from ash, and lime from limestone, would provide the glass batch. The major components of average glass containers in 1946 were reported by Moore and Lyle to be as follows, while in 1900 the average composition of window glass reported by Sharp was:

	1946	1900
Silica	72.1%	71.5%
Alumina	1.8%	1.5%
Alkaline Earths	9.8%	13.0%
Alkalies	15.6%	14.0%

In addition to this solution, Ravenscroft, in England, found another additive which would provide a durable glass. He added lead oxide to alkali and sand and came up with the formula for lead or "crystal" glass. A big advantage of the lead oxide addition was that the glass was made quite low melting. It also had a very high refractive index, so that glass articles which were cut or engraved would have much more sparkle than a soda lime glass. Naturally it was also more expensive, but for the engravers this was a minor factor when so much labor was involved. The composition of a modern lead glass was reported by Hutchins and Harrington to be the following, while an old lead bottle glass was reported by Sharp to be:

	1966	1900
Silica	56%	63.0%
Alumina	1%	0.6%
Lead Oxide	29%	21.0%
Alkalies	13%	13.0%

The most interesting aspect of ash washing is the opposite direction which is taken by modern "art" potters. A modern potter washes his wood ash, but throws away the liquid containing the fluxing alkalies and saves the residue with the lime and coloring agents, in an action that is diametrically opposed to that of the ancient glass makers!

Courtesy of the Corning Museum of Glass

Figure 33.4 A goblet crizzled to the extent of causing fracture.

Courtesy of Thomas Clarkson.

Figure 34.1   Contemporary ash glazed covered jar.

34 ASH CONSTITUENT VOLATILITY

The primary reason for loss of materials from ash glazes will be diffusion, such as the movement of solubles into the porous body when a glaze slip is applied, and the further diffusion of alkalies into and out of the body during heat treatment. However, there also has to be concern about **volatility** of ash constituents as firing progresses.

If we look at a list of the elements in ash, we can be concerned about the volatility of sodium and potassium and perhaps phosphate and sulfate, and surely chloride and associated cations.

First let us consider the alkalies, for it is obvious that something such as potassium or sodium chloride could be volatilized from a glaze, since we know that salt glazing with sodium chloride is a viable technique. On the other hand, sodium and potassium chlorides are not **that** volatile. Perhaps something in the range of one tenth of the alkali chlorides might be lost due to volatility, but this is not a significant amount, so we do not have to worry too much about losing alkalies.

Next, at high temperatures, in reduction, and in the presence of silica, we can also worry about the loss of phosphates. This is because they can be reduced to phosphides with a subsequent volatilization of phosphorus. Such a reaction apparently takes place in phosphate-containing glazes, as can be seen in Chinese Chun ware, where a bubbling occurs that is probably due to the evolution of phosphorus from the glaze. This does not seem to be a problem in wood ash glazes though. One seldom sees a large amount of bubbling at the surface of ash glazes since they are normally high in lime and this may have a stabilizing effect on phosphates.

Similarly with sulfates. We tend to think of sulfates as decomposing at high temperatures, giving off sulfur oxides and causing frothing in both glasses and glazes. But although there are sizable amounts of sulfate in almost every type of ash, the actual formation of ash glazes does not reveal this to be a problem. Since I have never noticed any frothing, I do not worry about sulfates.

Undoubtedly the most important element from a volatility standpoint is chloride. This loss occurs through the volatilization of alkali halides and through the loss of iron chlorides. In the latter case we may consider both the iron in the body and the iron in the glaze. If we think of a reduction firing, where iron is reduced to the divalent, ferrous form, then we may expect a loss of iron as ferrous chloride, which has a low boiling point. The appearance of highly colored iron deposits on the body just below the glaze may be an indication of the reoxidation of iron to the ferric state, while the bleaching of the body underneath the glaze-body interface, may be the true indication of the actual of loss of iron from both the glaze and the body. Apparently iron is most readily lost from the body rather than the glaze, because the celadon color does not seem to be affected. The body, on the other hand, does seem to show wide swings from the bleached areas to the deep brown varnished areas. This iron dispersal is the most striking evidence we have for volatilization in ash glazes.

Without doubt there is also a volatility loss of alkali halides from ash glazes. However, since alkali halides are not colored, there is no way to observe the loss. Furthermore, since there is normally a large excess of alkali vis-a-vis chloride, this is just a minor problem and we can ignore this aspect of halide loss.

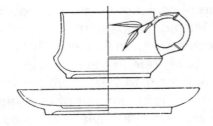

35 CONCLUSION

One of the most important things to learn from this collection of information is that you do not need ash to make an ash glaze. Just take a finely ground local shale or clay, or a commercial clay of this type such as Albany slip clay or Redart clay, and load it up with whiting (20-50%). Fire these test glazes to cone 8-10 on a sample piece, and behold! You've got an "ash" glaze.

Then your real work will begin. You will have to make decisions about color and run-off and body type, etc. And most important of all, you will have to decide if ash glazes are the right type of glaze for your style of living.

Pleasant Potting!

Ash tree about to be converted to an ash glaze.

BIBLIOGRAPHY

Anon., CLAYS AND SHALES OF NEW YORK - N.Y. Comm. Dept., 1951.

Anon., GRASS - US Govt. Printing Office, 1948.

Azzaro, Samuel, ASH GLAZES - MFA Thesis, Alfred University, 1969.

Ball, F. Carlton & Lovoos, Janice, MAKING POTTERY WITHOUT A WHEEL - Reinhold, 1965.

Beck, Charles, STONEWARE GLAZES - Isles House, 1973

Behrens, Richard, CERAMIC GLAZEMAKING - Ash Glazes, p. 30, 1976.

Behrens, Richard, GLAZE PROJECTS - Cement Glazes, p. 55, 1971.

Brankston, A.D., AN EXCURSION TO CHING-TE-CHEN & CHI-AN-FU - Trans. Oriental Cer. Soc., 1939.

Brill, R.H., THE SCIENTIFIC INVESTIGATION OF ANCIENT GLASSES - 8th Int. Congress on Glass, 1968.

Brill, R.H., INCIPIENT CRIZZLING IN GLASS - Bull. Int. Inst. for Conservation, **12**, 1972.

Chase, W.T., COMPARATIVE ANALYSIS OF ARCHEOLOGICAL BRONZES - in Archaeological Chemistry - Vol. 1, 1973

Chen Xianqiu, et al., DISCOVERY OF PHASE SEPARATION IN TEMMOKU GLAZES - (in Chinese), Shanghai, 1979.

Clarke, F.W., DATA OF GEOCHEMISTRY - Dept. of Interior, 1920.

Clarkson, Thomas, - Contemporary Clay, 3680 Stockton Road, Charlottesville, Virginia 22901.

Currie, Ian, STONEWARE GLAZES - Bootstrap Press, Maryvale, Q'ld, 4370, Australia, 1986.

Brother Daniel, L'ARTE DE CENDRES - (in French), Taizé Press, Taizé 71460, France, 1976.

Frasché, Dean, SOUTHEAST ASIAN CERAMICS - Asia Society, 1976.

192

Geilmann, Wilhelm, THE CHEMICAL COMPOSITION OF OLD GLASSES - Glastechn. Ber. (in German), **27**, p. 146-156. 1954.

Grebanier, Joseph, CHINESE STONEWARE GLAZES - Watson-Guptill, 1975.

Green, David, UNDERSTANDING POTTERY GLAZES - Faber, 1963.

Grim, R.E., CLAY MINEROLOGY - McGraw-Hill, 1968.

Hetherington, A.L., CHINESE CERAMIC GLAZES - Cambridge, 1937.

Kingery, W.D., & Vandiver, Pamela B., CERAMIC MASTERPIECES - Macmillan, 1986.

Leach, Bernard, A POTTER'S BOOK - Faber, 1945.

Lee, Jean Gordon, PHILADELPHIANS AND THE CHINA TRADE - Philadelphia Museum of Art, 1984.

Li Jiazhi, et al., SCIENTIFIC ACHIEVEMENTS IN ANCIENT CHINESE PORCELAIN - (in Chinese), Shanghai, 1986.

Ling, Meng-Chang, CHINESE ASH GLAZE - Bull. Am. Cer. Soc., **26**, p. 7-8, 1947.

Medley, Margaret, THE CHINESE POTTER - Phaidon, 1976.

Moes, Robert, MINGEI: JAPANESE FOLK ART - Universe, 1985.

Nelson, Glenn C., CERAMICS - Reinhart, 1960.

Palmgren, Nils, SUNG SHERDS - Almqvist, Stockholm, 1963.

Rawson, Jessica, CHINESE ORNAMENT - Brit. Mus., London, 1984.

Rhodes, Daniel, CLAY AND GLAZES FOR THE POTTER - Chilton, 1957.

Sanders, Herbert, THE WORLD OF JAPANESE CERAMICS - Kodansha, 1967.

Sato, Mashahiko, CHINESE CERAMICS - Weatherhill, 1981.

Thorpe, T. E., DICTIONARY OF APPLIED CHEMISTRY - p. 508-9, 1937.

Thurn, H. L., WOOD ASH IN A LOW-FIRE GLAZE - J. Am. Cer. Soc., **28**, p. 261, 1945.

Tichane, R.M., CHING-TE-CHEN: VIEWS OF A PORCELAIN CITY - NYS IGR, 1983.

Tichane, R.M., REDS, REDS, COPPER REDS - NYS IGR, 1985

Tichane, R.M., THOSE CELADON BLUES - NYS IGR, 1978.

Turner, W.E.S., STUDIES IN ANCIENT GLASSES - J. Soc. Glass Tech., **40**, 277T, 1956.

Valenstein, Suzanne, A HANDBOOK OF CHINESE CERAMICS - Metropolitan Museum of Art, 1975.

Wolff, Emil, ASCHEN ANALYSEN - (in German), 2 Vol., 1880, Berlin.

Wood, Nigel, ORIENTAL GLAZES - Watson-Guptill, 1978.

Azzaro, Samuel, ASH GLAZES - MFA Thesis, Alfred University, 1969.

Broadwell, Carolyn, ASH GLAZED PORCELAIN - MA Thesis, Colorado State College, 1969.

Glover, Bessie Irene, CONE TEN ASH GLAZES - MA Thesis, Eastern Carolina University, 1966.

Green Kenneth M., ASH GLAZES - MFA Thesis, University of Iowa, 1957.

Haefer, Curtis D., WOOD ASHES IN CONE TEN GLAZES - MA Thesis, University of Puget Sound, 1973.

Hysong, Joseph L., PLANT ASH GLAZES, MA Thesis, San Jose State University, 1962.

Johns, Donald A., SELECTED ASHES AS GLAZE INGREDIENTS - MA Thesis, Northern Illinois University, 1963.

Persick, William T., WOOD ASH GLAZES - MA Thesis, Ohio State University, 1956.

Rockwell, Robert E., CORNCOB ASH AS A GLAZE MATERIAL - Ohio State University, 1951.

Titus, Zella Katona, WOOD ASHES IN HIGH FIRE GLAZES - MA Thesis, University of Denver, 1952.

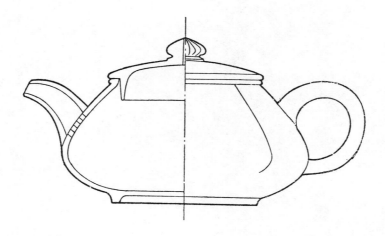

ASH GLAZE RECIPES

The following selected list of glaze recipes will have some notable omissions. A number of glazes with UNDEFINED ingredients have been left out. It is bad enough to try to make glazes from recipes containing "medium" ash, without trying to make a glaze from a recipe with an unspecified frit or weird stone. Just the normal variation in feldspars is enough to negate the results from many a glaze recipe. It would probably be best just to glance over this list of recipes and register a general feeling for ash glazes, instead of trying to duplicate any one recipe.

A further comment should be: in the various theses listed in the bibliography one can find literally hundreds of glaze recipes (many of which were unsatisfactory). The glazes selected from these works are the recipes which were recommended by the authors as the best of those tested.

Unless otherwise specified the glazes were fired in reduction.

Glazes Reported by Samuel Azzaro

Brown Glaze (cone 9-10):

Wood Ash	40
Albany Slip	60
Iron Oxide	5

Black Glaze (cone 9-10):

Wood Ash	20
Barnard Slip	60
Whiting	20

Tan Glaze (cone 9-10):

Wood Ash	65
Bone Ash	10
Dolomite	10
Talc	10

Brown Glaze (cone 9-10):

Wood Ash	40
Cornwall Stone	25
Albany Slip	20
Whiting	10
Iron Oxide	5

Warm Brown (cone 9-10):

Wood Ash	50
Dolomite	25
Flint	10
EPK	15

Golden Glaze (cone 9-10):

Wood Ash	52
Kaolin	15
Talc	12
Whiting	3
Bone Ash	1

Thin Golden Tan (cone 9-10):

Wood Ash	30
Soda Spar	30
EPK	30
Dolomite	25
Flint	10
Whiting	5

Carolyn Broadwell's Glazes

Gold Glaze II-3 (cone 9-10):

Washed Wood Ash	40
Albany Slip	60

Brown Glaze (cone 9-10):

Washed Wood Ash	20
Albany Slip	100
Barnard Slip	20

Glazes Reported by Brother Daniel

Transparent Cone 8 Glazes:

Oak Wood Ash	50
Kaolin	20
Silica	30

Oak Wood Ash	35
Kaolin	25
Silica	40

Opaque Cone 8 Glaze:

Oak Wood Ash	43
Kaolin	32
Silica	25

Glazes Reported by Bessie Glover

Cone 10 Glazes:

Hay Ash 40-60
Flint 20-25
Clay 5-10

Grebanier Glaze

Chun (cone 9-10):

Feldspar 56
Flint 22
Whiting 13
Wood Ash 9
Ochre 2.5

Glaze Reported by Curtis Haefer

Cone 10 Glaze:

Wood Ash 75
Feldspar 15
Kaolin 10

Glaze Reported by Donald Johns

Cone 8 Glaze:

Wood Ash 50
Albany Slip 50

Glazes Reported by Bernard Leach

Kawai Korean Type (cone 7-10):

Feldspar 25
Wood Ash 32
Reed Ash 17
China Clay 25
Iron Oxide 1.5

Kenzan Celadon (cone 7-9):

Feldspar 62
Wood Ash 18
China Clay 12
Quartz 2
Calcined Ochre 6
Iron Oxide 0.12

Hamada's Celadon (cone 6-8):

Feldspar 64
Pine Ash 27
Calc. Ochre 9

Tea Dust (cone 8):

Raw Ochre 50
Wood Ash 50

Kaki (8-11):

Feldspar 43
Wood Ash 30
Quartz 10
Iron Oxide 17

Hamada Kaki (cone 8-11):

Feldspar 33
Wood Ash 33
Reed Ash 25
Iron Oxide 9

Leach Ordinary Glaze (cone 8):

Feldspar 70   70   60
Wood Ash 20   30   30
Limestone 10   —   10

Leach Chun Glaze (cone 8-10):

Feldspar	58	55	30
Wood Ash	21	15	40
Reed Ash	16	25	30
Limestone	5	5	—

Glenn Nelson Ash Glaze

Cone 8 Semi-matte:

Feldspar	40
Wood Ash	40
Ball Clay	20

Glazes Reported by William Persick

Semi-matt Cone 8 Reduction Glazes:

Wood Ash	30
Jordan Clay	70
Colorant	1-5

Daniel Rhodes Glazes

Stony Matte Glaze (cone 9-10):

Wood Ash	35
Feldspar	35
China Clay	15
Talc	15

Satin Matte Glaze (cone 9-10):

Wood Ash	20
Dolomite	15
Flint	20
Feldspar	35
China Clay	10

Glazes Reported by Robert Rockwell

All Cone 8

Brown Base Glaze:

Corncob Ash	32
Feldspar	25
Albany Slip	44

Transparent Glaze:

Corncob Ash	28
Feldspar	22
Dolomite	11
Cornwall Stone	22
E.P.K	16

Brown Overglaze:

Corncob Ash	31
Feldspar	44
Barnard Slip	25

Black Overglaze:

Corncob Ash	25
Feldspar	50
Umber	25

Black Overglaze:

Corncob Ash	50
Feldspar	25
Umber	25

Black Overglaze:

Corncob Ash	22
Feldspar	37
Umber	19
Dolomite	3
Cornwall Stone	19

Sanders Temmoku Glazes

Cone 9-10 Glaze:

Albany Slip 50
Wood Ash. 10
Barnard Slip 10

Cone 9-10 Glaze:

Albany Slip 50
Wood Ash. 10
Iron Oxide 10

Glaze Reported by Zella Titus

Cone 9-10 Glaze:

Wood Ash. 50
Neph. Syenite 50
(or Feldspar)

Obviously there are many other ash glazes in the literature that have been inadvertently omitted here. However, many of the glazes that have been noted seem to revolve around a common theme, namely that of about half ash and half slip clay. Therefore the selection of a suitable glaze is closely tied to the particular ash available and the particular local clay available. Working on such a base, one can then choose additives such as colorants or aluminous materials that will fit a particular application.

ANALYSES

	*Si	Al	K	Na	Ca	Mg	Fe	Mn	Ti	P	Cl	LOI
EARTH'S CRUST	59.8	14.9	3.0	3.3	4.9	3.7	6.1	—	0.8	0.3	—	—
GRANITE (AVE.)	74.0	13.0	5.0	3.0	1.0	0.2	3.0	—	0.3	0.2	—	—
BASALT (AVE.)	52.0	14.0	1.2	3.2	9.3	6.4	12.8	—	1.0	0.4	—	—
SHALE (N.Y.)	64.6	15.4	3.3	0.6	0.6	2.0	7.2	—	0.9	—	—	3.9
REDART CLAY	64.3	16.4	4.1	0.4	0.2	1.6	7.0	—	1.1	—	—	4.8
ALBANY SLIP	59.5	11.5	2.8	0.4	6.3	3.4	4.1	0.1	0.9	—	—	10.4
BARNARD CLAY	52.4	10.6	4.0	—	—	—	20.3	3.2	0.9	—	—	8.3
FELDSPAR, SODA	66.8	19.7	4.5	7.0	1.8	—	—	—	—	—	—	—
FELDSPAR, POTASH	68.5	17.5	10.4	3.0	0.3	—	0.1	—	—	—	—	0.3
NEPH. SYENITE	60.3	23.3	5.1	10.6	0.3	—	0.1	—	—	—	—	0.4
CEMENT, PORTLAND	22.5	7.5	—	—	62.5	2.0	2.5	—	—	—	1.0	2.0
CHUN GLAZE	72.8	9.9	3.9	0.7	8.8	1.5	1.6	—	0.1	0.5	—	—
CHIEN TEMM. GLAZE	59.8	20.6	3.0	0.9	6.9	2.2	6.2	0.7	0.7	1.3	0.6	—

*Elements have been used as abbreviations for the oxides.

GLOSSARY

ACETIC ACID - The acid component of vinegar.

ACIDIC - In general, a material capable of neutralizing a base. At low temperatures acetic acid and boric acid are weak acids capable of neutralizing sodium carbonate. At high temperatures, silica is an acid capable of neutralizing lime (calcium oxide), etc.

ALBANY SLIP - A fine, natural, iron-containing clay capable of forming a dark brown glaze when fired to stoneware temperatures.

ALKALIES - Basic materials capable of reacting with acidic compounds to form neutral salts. The most commonly used alkalies in ceramic use are sodium, potassium and lithium compounds, such as sodium carbonate and potassium carbonate. The alkali elements are: lithium, sodium, potassium, rubidium and cesium. In ceramic reactions at high temperatures the alkalies act as fluxes when combining with silica.

ALKALINE EARTHS - The alkaline earth elements are: beryllium, magnesium, calcium, rubidium and barium. Their compounds with oxygen and carbon dioxide are capable of neutralizing acidic compounds to form neutral salts. The alkaline earth oxides and carbonates also act as fluxes when combining with silica at high temperatures.

BARNARD SLIP - A natural slip clay with a high iron content (20%) and a sizable manganese content (3%).

BASIC - The opposite of acidic; i.e., a material capable of reacting with an acidic compound to form a salt. Alkalies, such as sodium and potassium oxides and alkaline earths such as calcium and magnesium oxides are basic materials capable of reacting with the acid silica at high temperatures to form glasses, glazes or salts.

CALCINE - To take to a high temperature such as 1000°C for the purpose of removing water and other volatile material. Clay is sometimes calcined to reduce its drying shrinkage and ash is sometimes calcined to remove organic residues and water.

CALCIUM - Specifically "calcium" refers to the element, Ca. However, the term is often used loosely to refer to calcium oxide or calcium carbonate.

CALCIUM CARBONATE - Most accurately, calcium carbonate refers to the chemically pure compound ($CaCO_3$), but since naturally occurring material such as limestone is often quite pure, it can be considered to be synonymous with the latter.

CARBONATE - A compound formed from the reaction of an alkaline material such as sodium, potassium, calcium, or magnesium oxide, with the acidic gas carbon dioxide. The reaction of a carbonate with a stronger acid (such as acetic) will liberate carbon dioxide, a test used to identify carbonates.

CARBON DIOXIDE - A weakly acidic gas found to a slight extent (0.03%) in the atmosphere. Because of its ubiquitous occurrence, it will neutralize strongly basic compounds such as calcium oxide when they are stored in the air at ambient temperatures. It is a major component of furnace atmospheres when any carbonaceous material is used as a fuel. However, at high temperatures it is driven off compounds such as calcium carbonate.

CELADON - The common Western name for blue, blue-green or green glazes formed by the reduction firing of high temperature iron containing (about 1%) glazes.

CHI CHOU - The name for a Chinese ware of the Sung dynasty with a deep brown iron glaze decorated with ash splashes or patterns.

CHINESE CHRONOLOGY - Some of the important Chinese dynasties are:

SHANG - ca. 1500 - 1000 BC.
CHOU - ca. 1000 - 256 BC.
HAN - ca. 206 BC - 220 AD.
SIX DYNASTIES - 220 - 589 AD.
TANG - 618 - 906 AD.
SUNG - 960 - 1279 AD.
YUAN - 1279 - 1368 AD.
MING - 1368 - 1644 AD.
CHING - 1644 - 1912 AD.

CHING - The most recent (1644-1912) Chinese dynasty; noted among collectors and ceramists for the Kang-hsi (1662-1722) and Chien-lung (1736-1795) reigns, which were famous for their fine porcelain bodies and splendid glazes and decorations.

CHLORIDE - The negative ion in common salt. It is also found in ashes to a slight (0.1-1%) extent. However it is important because in its combination with iron, copper, sodium and potassium it leads to volatility of these elements during firing.

CHUN - The term for a Sung Chinese ware or glaze, normally a blue, opalescent celadon, that is occasionally decorated with splashes of copper red. The blue opalescence is partly caused by the phosphate content of the glaze, which could be from either plant ash or bone ash additions.

CLAYS - The naturally occurring fine platy minerals which are primarily hydrous alumino-silicates. Their most distinguishing feature is a plasticity when mixed with a limited amount of water. Clays are frequently contaminated with sizable quantities of iron, alkalies and alkaline earths.

CLINKER - A partially vitrified stony material. A slag.

COLEMANITE - The naturally occurring hydrated calcium borate. It is a sort of natural frit since it is rather insoluble and serves as an inexpensive source of non-leachable borate.

CRIZZLING - The degradation of glass through reaction with atmospheric moisture. It is a defect which used to occur in high alkali, silicate glasses which lacked other modifiers such as alumina, alkaline earths or lead oxides.

DEVITRIFICATION - A term indicating a loss of glassy characteristics due to the formation of fine crystals in a glass. It is used loosely to refer to crystallization in general, but it should be restricted to the high temperature transformation from a glassy condition to a mass containing crystals.

DOLOMITE - An alkaline earth mineral containing approximately one mole of magnesium carbonate for every mole of calcium carbonate. In making synthetic ash, this substance is a splendid inexpensive source of magnesium.

DURABILITY - That quality of glasses, glazes and other materials which defines their resistance to deterioration due to atmospheric or man-caused factors. It is a complex function of the chemical composition of glazes and glasses. Fortunately, in high fired glazes, the quantities of alumina which are used to furnish desirable viscosities will usually also provide good durability to natural weathering.

EDXR - Literally: Energy Dispersive X-Ray (analysis). This is a shorthand notation for the x-ray technique which allows a rapid **qualitative** elemental analysis of an inorganic sample. It is a splendid procedure for determining the approximate composition of an ash. Most scanning electron microscopes are now equipped with this type of instrument.

EQUIVALENT WEIGHT - The equivalent weight of an element is its atomic weight divided by its valence. The equivalent weight of a compound would be the mole weight divided by the valence of the appropriate element in the compound. For example: the equivalent weight of calcium would be 20 (1/2 of the atomic weight of 40). While the equivalent weight of calcium carbonate would be 50 (1/2 of the molecular weight of 100).

FELDSPARS - Alkali and/or alkaline earth alumino-silicate minerals with ideal properties for high temperature glaze formulations. In fact, feldspars are good glazes in themselves at sufficiently high temperatures. They are natural alkali sources with sufficient alumina for the formation of durable glazes.

FLINT - True flint is a microcrystalline form of silica, quite different in properties from quartz. It is usually not available in the United States. However, finely ground quartz is called "flint" by American potters. Both have the formula of silicon dioxide and if completely reacted in a glass or glaze, there will be no difference in the end result.

FLUX - A flux is a glaze ingredient which will react with other components of a glaze batch (usually glass formers such as silica) to form a glass. Such widely different compounds as lime, soda, boric oxide and lead oxide function as fluxes in glaze making.

GLASS - A glass is a non-crystalline solid at room temperature, and when fluid at higher temperatures it is characterized by its high viscosity. Glasses can become crystalline by holding them for extended periods just below their liquidus temperature. A glass is a supercooled liquid.

LIME - To be precise, lime is calcium oxide (CaO). However, the word is sometimes used loosely to describe limestone, calcium hydroxide, calcium, etc.

LIMESTONE - The mineral limestone (calcium carbonate or whiting), is frequently and widely found in a pure state, so there should be no contamination problem with this material; and it is a low cost ingredient.

MAGNESIA - Magnesia, the oxide of magnesium (MgO) is widely available, but the least expensive source of magnesia for glazes would be from dolomite.

MANGANESE - This element is normally available as the oxide (manganese dioxide) although it can be added to glazes as the carbonate (which is much more expensive). A problem with manganese dioxide is obtaining it in a pulverized form so that it can be well mixed with glaze batches.

MING - The Chinese dynasty (1368-1644) which first produced fine porcelain bodies on large scale. At that time the first great copper red glazes were made as well as some superb underglaze cobalt blue decorated ware.

MOLE - The mass in grams equal to the molecular weight of a substance. For example, calcium carbonate (whiting) has a molecular weight of 100 (Ca-40 + C-12 + 3xO = 48). Therefore a mole of calcium carbonate would be 100 grams.

OPALS - Opals in glasses or glazes usually are white, translucent materials. The opalescence is caused by light diffracting and scattering from particles, bubbles or droplets suspended in the glass. The suspended phase may be either a gas, a liquid (glass) or a crystal. A common opal in ash glazes is one liquid (a phosphate containing glass) suspended in another (the bulk glaze or silicate glass).

PEARL ASH - This is a name for potassium carbonate (sometimes in its crude form). Since this salt picks up moisture from the air very readily, its molecular weight may be hard to judge. Every effort should be made to keep it dry.

PH - The pH scale is a complex, but necessary, mathematical technique to quantify acidity and basicity. On the pH scale (running from 0-14), a pH of 1 would indicate that a solution was strongly acidic; a pH of 13 would indicate that a solution was strongly basic; a pH of 7 would indicate a neutral solution. The pH measurement can only be used in fairly dilute aqueous solutions. An unwashed wood ash slurry, for example, would probably have a pH of 12-13.

PHASE - A state of matter such as gas, liquid or solid.

PHASE SEPARATION - The parting of a single phase system into two or more immiscible phases. The usual difference in refractive index between any two phases commonly leads to opalescence or opacity of the resulting multi-phase system. A good example from life is the formation of fog in moisture laden air. In an ash glaze an example of phase separation would be the formation of an opal due to the separation of phosphate glass droplets in a cooling silica glass matrix.

PHOSPHATE - These are oxygen-containing negative ions with phosphorus as the central ion. The presence of a percent or so of calcium phosphate in a siliceous high temperature glaze will commonly lead to opal formation.

PHOSPHORUS PENTOXIDE - This is the simple oxide molecule containing two phosphorus atoms and five oxygen atoms. This compound is quite volatile at kiln temperatures. However when phosphorus pentoxide has reacted with calcium oxide it is stable at high temperatures (consider "bone" china).

PORCELAIN - In the West, porcelain is a ceramic which is high fired, translucent, resonant and white. However in the Orient it may be lacking in one or more of these properties. For example, Kuan ware of the Sung dynasty was considered to be "porcelain" even though it had a body which was dark colored, went "thunk" when struck and certainly wasn't translucent. Today, a severe critic might not even call it a stoneware. Nevertheless it was probably fired to at least 1200°C.

POTASH - The best definition of potash would be that it is potassium carbonate. However, potassium oxide is commonly referred to as potash also.

POTASSIUM - Potassium definitely refers to the element, but again, it is sometimes loosely used to refer to potassium oxide.

POTTERY - This is a category of ceramics which roughly covers all non-technical types. As a specific name it normally is used to describe those ceramic pieces which have been fired to temperatures below 1200°C and which are non-translucent.

PROTO-PORCELAIN - This a loose but useful category defining those Oriental ceramics preceding porcelain in development. Another definition of proto-porcelain would be "stoneware."

QUARTZ - The most common crystalline form of silica (silicon dioxide). This is the usual variety of silica purchased in the United States, but it may be called sand, "potter's flint," or rock crystal. Because quartz is hazardous to breathe, appropriate masks should be worn when working with this raw material.

QUICKLIME - This is calcium oxide (CaO). Also known as lime, this material is seldom used as a raw material, but it is an important intermediate during the thermal decomposition of calcium carbonate (whiting) before its reaction with other ingredients to form glazes. If wood ash is calcined above 900°C, then lime will be a major constituent of the product.

REDART - This is a trademarked name of the Cedar Heights Clay company for their brand of red clay. It contains about 7% iron oxide.

SILICA - Silica is the chemical name for the compound silicon dioxide (without reference to its physical form).

SLIP - A slip is a liquid suspension (usually aqueous) of the ingredients used to form either a body (by slip casting) or a glaze. The term is sometimes used loosely to identify a dry material used to make such a suspension, i.e., Albany slip (instead of Albany slip clay).

SODA - This term is mis-used so often that its original meaning is no longer valid. It once referred to the oxide of sodium, but it is commonly used casually to refer to sodium and its compounds in a general way.

SODA ASH - This is the anhydrous normal sodium carbonate. One should be aware of the fact that sodium carbonate is frequently hydrated and in this form is much more dilute than in the anhydrous state. For example, washing soda, the deca-hydrate, contains less than 50% sodium carbonate.

SODIUM - Accurately, sodium means specifically the element. Unfortunately I often use this name to refer to sodium oxide or soda.

SPAR - This is a shorthand term for feldspar, usually a potash feldspar.

STONEWARE - Stoneware clays are plastic materials used to make high-fired bodies. Stoneware bodies are not translucent and are usually greyer than porcelain. They are normally resonant though. The term most accurately describes some of the early high-fired Chinese "porcelains" or proto-porcelains.

SULFUR TRIOXIDE - When a sulfate reacts with an acid at high temperatures sulfur trioxide (or sulfur dioxide) is formed. These gases are the cause of some undesirable bubbles in glazes and bodies when extraneous sulfate in a batch reacts with the acid, silicon dioxide, at glaze-forming temperatures.

SUNG - One of the dynasties that produced classic Chinese ceramics was the Sung (960-1279 AD). It is noted for its thick, unctuous, blue and blue-green celadon glazes. Although the ceramics of this period are often called porcelains, a more accurate description would be stonewares.

TAIZÉ - Taizé is a hamlet 200 miles south of Paris, France, which is the site for a religious community of about 80 monks. One of the trades practiced there is ceramics, at which craft Brother Daniel works.

TEMMOKU - Once a specific term for the dark, brown-glazed wares of Chien, the term is now loosely applied (especially in the United States) to any dark brown glaze or ware.

TITANIUM - Titanium is an element close to iron in the periodic table. Titania, the dioxide, is commonly found at a level of 1-2% in ordinary earth and clays and is sold in concentrated form as the mineral rutile, anatase or brookite. Because of its interaction with iron, it has important consequences as a colorant in glazes and bodies. Titania's presence in celadon glazes leads to greener colors.

VINEGAR - This is the dilute acid (acetic) formed from the oxidation of wine or cider.

WET CHEMISTRY - A term describing a technique of chemical analysis in which chemical reactions such as oxidation-reduction, acid-base titration, or precipitation are used to analyze the ingredients in a mixture or compound.

WHITING - The common ceramic term for calcium carbonate (limestone).

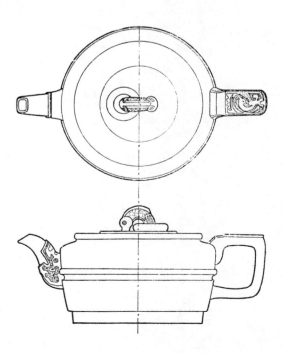

INDEX

*Numerals enclosed in parentheses
indicate illustrations.